Crazy About Quilting

CRAZY ABOUT QUILTING

Confessions of an Average Quilter

Ada K. Moyles

whitecap

For additional information, contact
Whitecap Books Ltd., 351 Lynn Avenue,
North Vancouver, BC V7J 2C4.
Visit our website at www.whitecap.ca.

EDITED BY Elaine Jones
PROOFREAD BY Marilyn Bittman
INTERIOR DESIGN BY Five Seventeen

LIBRARY AND ARCHIVES CANADA
CATALOGUING IN PUBLICATION

Moyles, Ada K.
Crazy about quilting / Ada K. Moyles.

ISBN 1-55285-758-1
ISBN 978-1-55285-758-8

1. Quilting—Anecdotes. 2. Quiltmakers—Anecdotes.
I. Title.

TT835.M69 2006   746.46   C2006-900705-5

The publisher acknowledges the support of the Canada Council for the
Arts and the Cultural Services Branch of the Government of British
Columbia for our publishing program. We acknowledge the financial
support of the Government of Canada through the Book Publishing
Industry Development Program for our publishing activities.

ANCIENT FOREST
FRIENDLY

The inside pages of this book are 100% recycled, processed chlorine-
free paper with 40% post-consumer content. For more information, visit
Markets Initiative's website: www.oldgrowthfree.com.

Printed in Canada

To Gordon
my greatest encourager

&

Susan and Mike
Kathy and Mark
Lorie and Robert
who will inherit the quilts

Table of Contents

Introduction

$\mathscr{L}$ast autumn, my husband and I were traveling through Oregon on our way home from a visit to our daughter in California. Our route took us within 20 miles of the town of Sisters, well known for its annual Outdoor Quilt Show held each July; one of those events that any quilter, given the opportunity, would want to attend. After an overnight stop in the town of Bend, my husband generously offered to take me into Sisters to see what was there. However, this was October, early in the morning and, with company arriving within two days, I was anxious to reach home. I reasoned that without the show and accompanying activities, there would not be the same attraction and the quilt shop(s) would probably not even be open when we got there. So I decided we should defer visiting Sisters until another time.

But, in life, as in quilting, things don't always turn out as planned. Sometimes they turn out even better. We had driven for about 20 minutes, when I realized we were not on the highway we had intended to take, but, in fact, were approaching Sisters. Somewhere, we had both missed a sign that would have guided us to our intended route.

Although the stores were not yet open when we reached the town, I spotted The Stitchin' Post, the quilt shop that organizes the July event, and asked my husband to stop so I could take a look in the window, if nothing else. As I admired the window displays and gazed into the interior of the shop, I noticed some people inside. They, in turn, noticed me and before long the door was unlocked and I was invited inside. A happy half-hour ensued, while I browsed through the shop, exchanged quilting experiences with some of the staff and, of course, made some purchases to add to my fabric stash.

Such a serendipitous occurrence is just one example of the many happy experiences that have added another piece to the adventure in patchwork that has been mine. Just as in the familiar crazy quilt, there has been no preplanned pattern to my quilting adventures. I have moved from one project to the next and tried my hand at various types of quilting with no particular goal or object, other than to try something new, enjoy what I was doing and bring pleasure to those who would receive the quilts. Yet, on reflection, like the pieces of a crazy quilt, the experiences and pleasures derived from the art and craft I most enjoy have colored and embellished my life beyond any pattern or plan I could have foreseen and have led me into sharing my love of quilting with others through writing. This book is the latest adventure in what has been, like my visit to Sisters, a delightful, though unplanned, journey through the world of quilting.

In a way, this book is also a crazy quilt, quilting and writing having many similarities. Various small pieces, with their own individual colors, designs and textures, some previously published in *Quilt World* magazine, have been written from the scrap bag of my life as a quilter. I have put them together much as I did when piecing a crazy quilt, by starting with a focal point, adding to it until a unit has been completed, embellishing to enhance the block (or editing and adding photographs to enhance the written piece) and putting all the pieces together to produce what I hope will be, for the reader, a rich, colorful and pleasurable reading experience.

It's Not My Fault

$\mathcal{I}$ blame it on the encouragers, my addiction to quilting. For yes, I must admit it. I'm a quilt addict. Of course I knew that long ago, but, like many other addicts, refused to admit to my addiction. It wasn't until recently that it came out into the open.

On a winter holiday to the sunny south, when I had taken no quilting projects with me, the symptoms became obvious. After three weeks of a planned month's visit, I said to my husband one day, "I'm ready to go home now."

Eyeing me with his usual perception, (and even though I hadn't mentioned the "q" word) he said, "You can't stay away from your quilting, can you?"

Whereupon, I had to confess sadly, "No, I can't! I love it!"

But it's not my fault, I cried inwardly. It's the fault of the encouragers.

First, there was Carol, who introduced me to it. She called one day to see if I would be interested in taking a "quilting basics" course with her. She didn't drive, I did; so I could provide her with transportation to the classes. And as quilting was something I had always had an interest in—my mother and my namesake having been quilters—I agreed to take the course with her.

I now realize quilting was in my genes. One taste of it and I was inevitably destined to become a quiltaholic!

Well, to continue the sad story, one course led to another, and before I knew it I was making two quilts for the twin beds in my older daughter's room, followed immediately by two more for the bunk beds in my son's room. Thankfully, my younger daughter only had one bed in her room, but, of course, she had to have a quilt, too. There was only one more practical reason to make another quilt—for our own bed, and so I did.

By this time, I was hooked.

And somehow or other, like all addicts, I've been able to come up with excuses to justify my habit ever since. A new baby on the way? I'll make a quilt. A family wedding? A quilt would be a meaningful gift. A craft store nearby? Perhaps I could sell my quilts there. At least then I would be able to pay for my addiction without resorting to desperation financing, the ultimate downfall of many addicts.

Then, there was my husband. Yes, I'm sorry to say that he has to share the blame, too. If he hadn't admired my work and offered constructive criticisms when asked, perhaps I wouldn't be where I am today. Carol's husband, for example, didn't care for quilts. So she gave up quilting and, to fill her days, resorted to returning to university and earning her PhD. She's now a college professor, poor woman!

Friends, too, must bear some responsibility. When shown my quilts, they offered their own compliments and encouragement; occasionally even commissioning a quilt for themselves. Heady stuff. How could I refuse?

So you see, it's not really my fault that I enjoy quilting more than any other leisure activity that I can think of. If it hadn't been for those encouragers, I would never have bought all that beautiful fabric, taken all those interesting courses, read all those fascinating magazines, attended all those inspiring quilt shows, made all those new friends and become part of a whole new world.

Blessed are the encouragers!

Mrs. Average Quilter

$\mathcal{I}$t was confirmed once again as I filled out the application for the quilting class. I'm just an average quilter.

"Circle your level of expertise," the form read. "Beginner. Intermediate. Advanced."

Well, I certainly couldn't circle "Beginner." I've been quilting for over 20 years now. (Can it really have been so long?) And only a completely inept sewer could call herself a beginner after all that time. But "Advanced"? No. Definitely not.

Advanced quilters make all their stitches the same length on the front and on the back. I settle for *most* of the stitches being *almost* the same length, especially on the front.

Advanced quilters can spend hours at a time doing perfect machine stippling to highlight their latest creative effort. As for me, machine stippling and I made a brief acquaintance at a guild-sponsored quilting class and by mutual consent waved a happy "Goodbye" when the class was over.

Advanced quilters are in the forefront of the latest innovations in quilting. Their stained glass masterpieces were in shows a decade ago. My humble effort is less than halfway to completion and there is grave doubt at this point whether it will ever get beyond it. Their color-wash wall hangings were on display before the ink was dry on the books describing the technique. My color-wash technique is limited to fishing the red socks out of the laundry before they ruin the white T-shirts.

Advanced quilters call themselves "fiber artists" and wear gorgeous gowns made out of old neckties at those tony events to which we all know they are invited. My only claim to the title "fiber artist" is that I make my own granola!

Advanced quilters have their own TV shows. They are guest lecturers all over the continent. They go on quilting cruises to teach other advanced quilters new techniques.

No messages are left on my answering machine from TV producers, quilt show organizers or cruise directors.

Definitely average.

But you know, I like it that way.

I have no reputation that I feel obliged to live up to. No deadlines from galleries for completion of my latest works of art. Should I ever be lucky enough to go on a cruise, I could lie all day in my deck chair and enjoy the sun. I don't have to worry about taking slides to illustrate my lectures or entertain my guild. I can make what I like, when I like and it doesn't matter if I'm the only one who thinks it's a masterpiece.

Being average definitely has its advantages!

The Worst Quilt
in the World

$\mathcal{I}$own it. The Worst Quilt in the World. On a scale of one to ten this quilt would rate about minus 20. And what is more, I made it. Yes, I admit it.

This is a quilt that no self-respecting quilter would admit to owning, let alone to having made. But today I am bringing it out of the closet, so to speak, and for a very important reason.

But first of all, you need to know its history.

Remember polyester double-knit?

It was the miracle fabric of the seventies—cheap, sturdy, machine washable, easy to sew, comfortable to wear—at least if it didn't get too hot or too cold. Well, in the seventies we were a polyester double-knit family. My eight-year-old son was resplendent in polyester double-knit flares; bell-bottoms, the older generation called them. My five-year-old daughter had cute little dresses with hot pants (remember them?). I had a four-piece coordinating outfit of skirt, vest, pants and jacket in mix-and-match polyester double-knit patterns and plains. The latest thing in style. I even made my husband a polyester double-knit suit with a safari-style jacket, the in look of the seventies. He wore it, too!

So, with all that polyester double-knit around, there were lots of scraps. Now my Scot's blood told me you can't waste all that fabric. A polyester double-knit quilt would be just the thing. So I carefully laid square templates on the fabric, traced them round and, using scissors, cut out enough pieces for a quilt. (No rotary cutters then.) I sewed them together and made a not-too-bad-looking quilt—for polyester double-knit.

But I still had more fabric left.

Another quilt? Why not!

Having used up my none-too-abundant supply of patience on the first quilt, I decided there must be a quicker way. All that tracing around templates could be eliminated. Why couldn't I just cut out random rectangles and sew them together as I went? Much simpler and quicker, I thought. So I began. About halfway down the quilt I could see that it wasn't working out quite evenly. Polyester double-knit stretches and my quilt was gradually getting wider and wider. Still I persevered, until there came a point where I realized that something drastic was needed.

Take it apart and begin again? Out of the question!

Abandon it and waste all that time, effort and material? No way!

So, in a stroke of inspiration (or madness), I decided to even up the sides by cutting a wedge out of the middle. By the time I had used up most of the fabric, I was ready to admit that this quilt wasn't going to win any compliments. But, too stubborn to give up on it, I bought a cheap piece of polycotton for the backing, laid the batting and quilt top on it, folded the back over the front, stitched it together on the machine and threw it in a cupboard.

But the funniest thing about that quilt is that it has probably been one of the most useful quilts I've ever made. I never cared what happened to it, so it has gone on winter picnics and summer camping trips; it's been thrown on the patio deck for the kids to play or to suntan on; it's been wrapped around pots of soup to keep them warm in the car while traveling from one house to another and it's been wrapped around kids lying on the floor watching cartoons on Saturday mornings. And it never seems to wear out. Polyester double-knit appears to be indestructible.

Recently, as I spied that old quilt in the depths of the closet, I got to thinking. Maybe I should rename it. Perhaps it should be called the Most Useful Quilt in the World.

We're Moving Faster
But Can We Still See the Scenery?

$\mathscr{I}$t is one of the ironies of the modern quilting world that, in a day when there is absolutely no need for us to make quilts to warm our families, we are able to make them faster and with less effort than our foremothers, who made them from necessity.

Just think of the changes in the tools alone. What did our great-grandmother use to make her quilts? Scissors, a needle, thread, fabric. A thimble and a ruler if she were lucky. If not, any straight edge would do. And her fingers were often so hardened from her daily toil that a thimble would have been superfluous. But the quilts she produced were just as beautiful in their way as the masterpieces of the present day.

Then came the sewing machine. What a boon that must have been for the woman who didn't have enough hours in her day to keep up with all the demands on her time—farm, family, and sometimes hired men, for whose physical welfare she was often responsible. Oh, the joy of being able to sew up seam after seam in only seconds! Why, a quilt could be pieced that way in a fraction of the normal time. But, I wonder, did she miss the pleasure of joining each tiny piece by hand as she sat in the quiet of her kitchen after her family had all retired for the night, with only the glowing fire for company? Did she miss the peace of mind that descends when all is quiet and the mind is focused on the relaxing task at hand? Perhaps. But I believe she found even greater satisfaction in the hum of the machine and the way in which she could see her work take shape before her eyes.

Now we take the use of the sewing machine for granted and few of us take the time and effort to piece a whole quilt by hand, even though there is no necessity for it to be done in a hurry.

And the patterns we have.

Where our great-grandmothers carefully copied patterns shared at the quilting bee, or waited for the next issue of the *Ladies Art Company* catalog to be passed on from a friendly neighbor in order to see the newest pattern, we have books upon books of patterns and quilt magazines everywhere we look. Our minds are set awhirl by all the choices we see. All the patterns crying out to be tried. All the techniques waiting to be learned. All the tools, all the gadgets, all the materials. And we haven't even mentioned designing by computer.

Some days it seems almost too much!

It is then that we go back to the ways of the past. We get out our scissors and needles, our thimbles and thread and cut out a pretty little appliqué. We position it carefully on the square of background fabric and, like our great-grandmothers, we make one tiny stitch after another, until the frenzy of the modern world is replaced with the peace of the past. Our minds relax. Our hearts are lifted.

Thankfully there are some things that never change.

Show and Tell

$\mathscr{I}$finally did it. I took my quilt to our guild's show and tell.

Show and tell is one of the most popular features of our monthly guild meetings. In the auditorium where we meet, members bring their quilting projects and spread them out over the seats for other quilters to admire and be inspired by. At a particular point in the program the quilts are held aloft by two members, wearing the mandatory protective white gloves, and the quilt-maker is given an opportunity to say something about the article he (yes, we have men in our guild) or she has brought.

But, for the average quilter, like myself, bringing a quilt to show and tell is like sending your child off to her first day of school. Will the other students like her? Will they admire her dark brown eyes and cute little smile or only notice her scraped knees? Will the teacher see how clever she really is?

Will the other members like my quilt? Will they notice my innovative design and careful choice of colors? Or will they only notice that not all my points are perfect?

I take it out of its green plastic bag. (This looks really tacky. Next project: make a proper quilt carrier.)

"What have we here?" a cheerful voice asks.

I carefully spread my quilt over the seats and wait apprehensively for the reaction.

"It's lovely," the same voice comments.

Several ladies gather round and ask questions about the pattern.

"Did you design it yourself? I've never seen a quilt like it before."

I reply that my quilt is my own design based on an idea I saw elsewhere.

"Very creative."

I try not to look too proud.

At show and tell time, I say my piece about the reasons for making the quilt and the applause that follows is gratifying.

But the real accolade comes later in the week.

The phone rings and a voice says, "I saw your quilt at the last guild meeting and I would like to incorporate some of your ideas in my next project. Would you mind? And do you think I could see the quilt once more?"

Of course you can, dear lady. Come on over and I'll put the kettle on. We'll have a cup of tea and I'll tell you all about it.

On a Roll

It really all started with Mary Ellen Hopkins.

She was the guest at our guild's tenth anniversary and that's when I bought her book: *The It's OK If You Sit on My Quilt Book*. During the intervening years I have referred to it now and then, when I was looking for a particular block or block name, or for inspiration for the next project. It has become for me, as I'm sure it has for many people, a standard source of ideas.

One of my favorite stages in the making of a quilt is the design process. I love to play around with graph paper, ruler and colored pencils. I know there are computer programs that let you do this a lot faster, but it's something like comparing machine quilting and hand quilting. It's the process, as well as the outcome, that's pleasurable. For me this is an inexpensive substitute for making a quilt. Moreover, if the ideas seem less than inspired when put on paper, you can chuck the whole thing and start all over, literally with a clean sheet.

So that's what I was doing when the ball started to roll. Playing with an idea. Not an original one, I know, but it was new to me. I began with a simple little block that in Mary Ellen's book is called Crosses and Losses. This little block is made up of two basic elements: a square made up of two right-angle triangles and another four-patch square consisting of two smaller two-triangle squares and two plain squares. I decided to see what combinations I could make using these basic elements.

I was hoping to come up with four interesting variations, which I would separate with sashing in a small wall hanging or a miniature sampler quilt, perhaps. A fairly quick, simple project. Or so I thought.

I limited myself to using each unit eight times, making a sixteen-patch block. I also limited myself to three colors—two strong complementary colors to emphasize the patterns and a more muted background shade. To limit the possibilities even further, I decided that the color arrangement would always be the same in each basic unit.

The first four variations came so easily that I decided to carry on with the idea and see how many arrangements I could come up with. An hour later it was clear this would have to be at least an eight-block project. And, I thought, that's probably all the variations there are. A mathematician could have told me exactly how many permutations and combinations were possible, but that would take the fun away. I prefer to be surprised.

The project got put on hold for a while, but when I went back to it, with a fresh eye and uninterrupted time for experimenting, I began to see more and more pattern possibilities. This has got to be a small quilt, at least, I thought, as the fifteenth variation unfolded on the paper.

Now, what had Mary Ellen said about other patterns emerging? Supposing I put two of the same blocks side by side. Yes, there would be another different pattern. In fact, just that one arrangement repeated would make a striking quilt all by itself. (Of course, I would have to make that *after* the sampler.) And so would this next block. And that one, too.

Just supposing I changed the color arrangement in the basic units. Wow! That would open up another world of options. There must be dozens of quilts here. I could probably produce a book based on just that one little pattern.

I know. I know. I probably never will. But I had a lot of fun with the idea.

Thank you, Mary Ellen Hopkins.

A Natural Combination

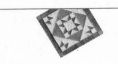

There is something about babies and baby quilts that makes them a natural combination. Perhaps it's because both are small, easily carried around, cozy and made with love!

How many quilters have made their first quilt for a baby, I wonder?

Quilting is such an ancient art that it was even known to the early Egyptians.

Did Moses' mother learn how to quilt when she lived in Egypt? I'm sure that when she tucked him into the little reed basket, she would have covered him with a blanket to comfort him and protect him from the cool river air. Perhaps, when Pharaoh's daughter saw how lovingly he was cared for, her heart was moved to love and protect him herself. And if Moses' mother didn't already know how to quilt, it is quite possible that, as the care-giver for her son in the court of the Pharaohs, she encountered Egyptian women with their fabric and needle, making quilted garments for the courtiers.

As her son was being raised to be the companion of a future Pharaoh, naturally she wanted him to look his best. A hand-quilted garment would let everyone know that he was a person of some importance.

Since those long-ago days, I venture to guess, there have been few quilters who have not lovingly chosen the fabrics and pattern and carefully stitched a quilt for a special baby.

I made my first one as a shower gift for a young friend, who was expecting her first baby. The quilt featured appliquéd teddy bears in blue and yellow trousers sporting blue bow ties. It was a very simple pattern but looked fresh and pretty when finished off with white eyelet lace around the border.

My friend was delighted with the quilt and I thought no more about it until quite a few years later, when she (having had two more children in the meantime) casually mentioned how much she loved the quilt I had made for her first baby and bemoaned the fact that, as a result of being used to cuddle each of the three children, it was now getting very well worn. These indications that one's efforts have been so valued bring joy to a quilter's heart.

Since then, I've made quilts for many babies—for family members, as shower gifts, for charity sales, or simply as a change from larger projects. They have traveled with their owners to various parts of Canada and the United States. One, I recently discovered, had been literally loved to pieces and I took pity on its now six-year-old owner (who wouldn't be parted from the tattered remains) and made her another just like the original. Others have been hung on nursery walls and later, carefully packed away, to be saved for the babies when they are grown. All have been treasured by their recipients.

It is pleasant to think that, many years from now, perhaps long after I have gone, someone, somewhere, will look at their little baby quilt and wonder about the woman who made it for them.

I hope they will see that the quilt-maker enjoyed her work; that they were loved and protected; that, even when they were little, they were considered a person of some importance; and, that stitched into each quilt were many good wishes for their well-being.

Make My Day!

"*T*urn around."

The somewhat demanding tone of the voice startled me.

I was standing in line in an airport washroom, wearing a jacket I had made from old denim jeans and various scraps of ribbon, bias tape and other odds and ends. It was the end product of a workshop I had attended on making vests from old denim.

Not being a jeans wearer myself, I needed to get a good supply of various types of denim to begin the project and begged old castoffs from my adult children. Local thrift stores were also prime targets and I was lucky enough to visit one when they had a special promotion—everything you could put into the bag they provided, for a nominal cost. They must have thought I had an awfully big husband as I went for the racks with the extra-large sizes. A real bonanza! That got me through the first couple of vests, but I wasn't finished with the idea yet, as a jacket seemed to be the next logical step. So, weekends found me bargaining shamelessly at garage sales at the end of the day for jeans no one else seemed to want. Taking pity on this obviously cash-strapped woman (or else seeing me as their only hope of getting rid of stuff they really didn't want to have to pack back into the house) they let me recycle their "experienced" jeans at well below garage sale price.

Now that I had the denim I had to decide on a jacket style. Could I find a pattern to adapt?

I settled on a simple, shirt-style jacket with turned-back collar and buttoned cuffs. Days went by as I cut and re-cut; matched and re-matched, stitched and re-stitched, trying to settle on just the right look.

Finally, it was done. But would I ever wear it?

It was unlike most of my (pretty ordinary) clothing that I didn't know how comfortable I'd feel in it. But denim is a forgiving fabric. You can throw it down in a heap, or stow it in a cupboard and it doesn't show wrinkles or complain of neglect. There were so many different shades of blue, gray and black in the jacket that, while it didn't actually match anything, it didn't clash with anything either (as long as it was blue, gray or black!), so that it turned out to be an ideal travel jacket. That's why I was wearing it when I was accosted by the voice.

Turning around as I had been ordered, I looked into the smiling face of the woman next in line. Seeing my startled expression, and perhaps realizing how abrupt she had sounded, she smiled at me and said, "I've been admiring the back of your jacket and I just wanted to see the front."

Instantly, all was understood.

Had I made it myself?

Yes, I had.

Did I make them to sell, or just this one?

Sell? (Lady, if you knew how much effort this had cost me, you wouldn't ask me that.) Oh, no. I just made this one and a couple of vests, I had to add, just to let her know it wasn't merely a lucky try.

Well, you certainly did a good job. It's very striking.

Thank you, very much.

By this time I was at the head of the line and the conversation ended.

But I was reminded of a previous occasion when I was stopped in a park by another lady who asked if I had made the quilted jacket I was wearing. It turned out she was also a quilter and for a few moments we shared a little conversation before we went our separate ways.

Both these encounters left me with a warm glow. I enjoy my hobby. I think what I make is fine, most of the time (although I admit there's always room for improvement), but it is good to have that confirmation from others.

So, when you see someone wearing a unique garment you admire, which she quite possibly made herself, tell her you like it.

It will make her day.

Looking Ahead

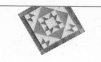

For those readers on the sunny side of 40, a warning: Read No Further!

The following may contain disturbing material; reader discretion is advised; may contain scenes of graphic vio—— Okay. It's not really that bad. But remember, you have been warned.

For as someone once told me, "Growing old is not for the faint of heart."

Yes, growing old. Today's pop culture would like us to believe that no one really grows old. Or, if they do, they merely have more time to enjoy all the benefits of their wisely invested money, either on the golf courses of their newly acquired exclusive condominiums, or cruising in the warm waters of the Caribbean, or other equally salubrious locations, surrounded by similarly ageless people.

What is seldom portrayed are the aches and pains, the gradual diminishing of abilities which will come to all of us, with the occasional rare exceptions, as we live longer and spend many more years in retirement than any previous generation.

What drew my thoughts in this somewhat depressing direction was the ache that appeared in my neck after a recent sewing binge. Working to a deadline to produce some costumes for a daughter's forthcoming musical production, I was spending more hours at the sewing machine than I usually do at one time. I knew I was overdoing it, but thought, "Oh, that ache will disappear when I rest for a day or two after I finish."

Yes, it did. But the next time I began sewing, there it was again. Even after a three-week vacation from the sewing machine, as soon as I started sewing again, it was back, just enough to let me know that my body wasn't able to shake off the strains and tensions of prolonged work as it once had.

Of course, that wasn't the first indication I had that I was no different from the rest of the human race. I first became aware of the advancing years one day when I was getting perilously close to the big five-o and, looking at my hands, suddenly realized that these were the hands of a middle-aged woman.

Not too long after came the need for bifocals, then trifocals. Now I have three pairs of glasses and there are still times when I have to take off whatever pair I am wearing in order to complete the task at hand.

Then there's ... but enough of this.

If you, like me, qualify for the seniors' discount at hotels and restaurants, you know all too well what I am talking about. And if you are under 40 and ignored the warning previously given, you really don't want to hear any more, do you?

So, in case I've depressed you with these rambling thoughts, let me tell you some of the good things about getting older. And, yes, there are many good things!

Although I can't spend as long at any one quilting task as I used to, that's okay. Because with no offspring living at home, I have lots more time to do whatever I like. So I don't need those marathon weekends, or the late-night "got-to-get-this-finished" sewing sessions. (With the occasional exception, as already mentioned!)

Also, with my children on their own—at least living in their own homes—I no longer have to compete for sewing space on the kitchen table with homework, play-dough art or family meals. And I now have not only a spare bedroom but, joy of joys, my own sewing workroom.

Having been quilting for quite some years, in addition to the quilts I use and have kept, I have built up a respectable collection of photographs of completed projects that now have other owners. Add to that the joy quilting has given me over the years and still is giving, the things I have learned and am still learning, the friends I have made and am still making, the visits to and memories of delightful quilt shows, and the opportunities to share the love of quilting with younger quilters, and it seems that the occasional reminder of my humanity is a small price to pay.

And one more thing.

Through quilting, I have made several friends who have been quilting for most of their long lifetimes, alongside whom I am still a novice with years of enjoyment ahead of me. Friends like Ruby, not only friend but mentor, who began quilting when she was 12 years old. Until well into her eighties, with sight in only one eye and the care of a husband suffering from Alzheimer's disease, she regularly entered all the challenges of our guild and produced not only highly acceptable work, but continued to show creativity and learn new techniques as the opportunities arose.

Such quilters inspire me to keep looking forward to my next project. And if, as someone has said, "A quilter's heaven is where you get to make all the quilts you didn't have time for on earth," there's really no end of quilting pleasures to come.

There. I feel a whole lot better already.

The Dud

$\mathcal{I}$ hate to admit it but it's true. I've made a dud. Like a firecracker that fails to ignite, this quilt does nothing for the eye. In spite of my best efforts at design, fabric selection and construction, this quilt is definitely a Dud with a capital D! Even my family, who are so supportive, can only shake their heads in sympathy and agree that they don't like it either.

It's not that it's badly made, or ugly (well, perhaps just a little); it's just that none of us likes it. And that really bothers me.

I've put a lot of thought, time and effort, not to mention money, into this quilt and to have it turn out so badly—it's enough to make you want to cry.

You see, this was a major project: a queen-sized cover planned to replace the bedspread in our room. That well-worn quilt, while it looked so fresh and up-to-date when I made it, with its peach and green color scheme, had lost its appeal. To my eyes at least, it was ready to be replaced.

Isn't it funny how colors and designs that seem so striking when we first see them, lose their charm over the years and as time passes seem positively unattractive? Remember harvest gold and avocado green kitchen appliances?

But back to the Dud.

I thought a lot about the design. It had to be something different from the old quilt, but within my capabilities to actually finish. I decided on a star motif and after a number of happy hours with pencils, ruler, erasers and graph paper came up with a design that I thought would fit the bill and the bed. In retrospect it would have been better to choose a pattern and color scheme from a pattern book and just make a copy. But then the quilt wouldn't have been so much mine.

My design called for five or six different fabrics and off I went to make my selections. Taking every care to make sure my choices were good, I decided to purchase a small quantity of each fabric and make up a sample block on a smaller scale. Having cut the required pieces, I laid them on my design board and realized immediately that one of the fabrics just didn't suit the design. A number of other projects and activities intervened and by the time I had decided to go ahead with the star quilt, several months had passed by. So, as you might expect, when I went back to the fabric shop, with a somewhat simplified design, to purchase the fabric that was to be the basis of the quilt, there wasn't enough of it left on the bolt for my use.

Not to be deterred, however, I brought my adult daughter along on yet another fabric buying expedition to assist me with my color choices. Eventually I purchased what she and I thought would be a good combination for the quilt.

But, alas! As I cut the fabrics and laid them out side by side, there was none of that spark of enjoyment that comes when you know things are going well. Having gone so far, however, I thought, "Perhaps it will look okay on the bed" (major error!) and continued to piece and sew until I had the top just about completed, except for the borders.

Well, it didn't look any better in the room it was intended for than it had when I was sewing it. When my husband saw it, he said, very gently, "Well, I have to say I don't like it very much."

"Neither do I," I said sadly.

Together we discussed what might be done to improve and salvage the project. Change the fabric used here?

That could be done, though not without taking it all apart. Alter the borders? Maybe. Alternate star colors? A possibility, but I would have to purchase more of one fabric, if it were still available.

I was so determined to persevere, I picked the whole quilt top apart (I'm talking queen-sized spread, remember) and began to re-sew it into the altered design. But still no spark of life! With a sinking feeling, I laid the refinished quilt top on the bed and finally had to admit defeat. It was a minor improvement over the original, but still a dud.

It sits on a shelf in my sewing room now, unfinished, unusable, unlovely. A constant reminder of failure. I haven't the heart to finish it or to throw it out.

Any suggestions?

Metamorphosis
(or After the Dud)

$\mathcal{S}$o there I was facing the same problem. In spite of a valiant attempt I still didn't have the much-needed quilt for our bed. Star patterns still appealed to me and when I saw an interesting design using one star in four different sizes and only two colors, I thought it would be ideal.

The pattern was appealing because, first of all, it simplified the choice of fabrics. Which brings me to a confession. When it comes to choosing fabric, I am—how shall I put it—color handicapped? No, that suggests color-blindness. Pattern defective? No, it's not the patterns that I have difficulty with. It's just that making a definite choice is so final. Once the fabric is cut off the bolt, it's yours. There's no going back. I am fabric-challenged!

Normally, I like to think that I am a decisive person. A woman who can quickly weigh up options, sum up the pros and cons and make a wise choice. I can make instant and easy decisions in the supermarket. I can study a map and tell my husband what turnoff to take on a hitherto untraveled section of highway. I can read a restaurant menu and make my selection with alacrity; and if they had asked, (which, of course, they didn't) I could have told my children what paths to take in higher education and thereby saved them months, if not years, of time and effort, not to mention money.

If an elected politician ever phones me with a difficult problem, I have no doubt that, in a relatively short time, I could help her sort out the situation, outline her options, and direct her to the best solution. Even when buying something as important as a new house, I have been known to take less time to make a decision than it takes me to select fabric for a quilt.

That's why I find it so difficult to admit that when it comes to choosing fabric for quilts, I am an entirely different person. Something happens to me when I go through the doors of the fabric shop and, whatever it is, it means that I can be there for hours, looking at bolt after bolt and still come away empty-handed. Put me in front of a shelf full of fabric and my mind immediately goes into low gear, occasionally refusing to function at all.

So, this two-fabric pattern seemed ideal. I shouldn't have to spend hours debating the color scheme; deciding if this or that fabric was the better choice; enlisting the help of family, friends, sales assistants and even bystanders, as I have been known to do, before making my purchase.

Another plus was that the pattern was relatively simple to cut and piece. And the instructions were for a queen-sized quilt, which was exactly the size I needed. I wouldn't need to change a thing. This was going to be one of the easiest and quickest projects yet.

Little did I know!

Before starting the quilt, I decided that perhaps I should show the pattern to my husband. After all, he was going to have to look at it as much as I was, after it was on our bed, and that produced setback number one. He didn't care for the pattern at all. No amount of persuasion and suggesting that it would look quite different with different colors or pointing out the ease with which I could make it, changed his mind. He just didn't care for stars. End of quilt?

Well, not exactly. I don't give up that easily! However, I did let the idea simmer in my subconscious, while I got on with other projects.

It was a piece of fabric (chosen by my husband) in a fabric shop in Hawaii, that resurrected the idea. A lovely leaf print in a combination of colors ranging from soft greens, to gray-blues, to copper, to tan. I had no plan for its use when I bought it, so it was set aside and the design and colors slipped into my subconscious, and there with a cry of *Eureka!* met the discarded star pattern. Met, merged and metamorphosed into—not a star quilt, but a leaf quilt. A leaf quilt, full of life and energy, blending all sorts of fabrics with the whole gamut of colors in the original. I could use up all the accumulated autumn-tones fabric I had already. All I would need to buy was the background fabric, some sashing and perhaps small amounts of new fabrics to add more variety. It would be colorful, exciting and easy to do.

With my husband's agreement to the revised plan, like a racehorse when the gates open, I was off!

Modifying the original pattern, I kept the concept, but changed the design. Pulling fabrics from my stash, I selected and rejected, until my choices were settled. Happening on a fabric sale, I bought the background material, sashing and some additional coordinating colors.

As I cut and stacked the pieces, I happily imagined a new and exciting quilt.

But there was a lot more to come. Multi-fabric leaves were rejected in favor of each leaf being made of the same fabric. Opinions were sought from husband, family, friends and visitors—some from as far away as Australia. Changes were made in leaf arrangements and sashing design. Completed leaves were positioned and repositioned until we were happy with the final arrangement. Borders were added, which called for a decision on the quilting design. But finally, basted, quilted and bound, with label added, it was done.

The simple, two-color star pattern had evolved into a vibrant, colorful, eye-catching bed-cover. A completed quilt and a complete metamorphosis!

Back Issues

$\mathcal{I}$t all came back to me as a result of a phone call from my friend Ruby.

Ruby is my quilting mentor and inspiration. When I was a beginning quilter, I frequently called on Ruby for help and advice and she was always generous with her time and encouragement. Some years ago she gave me a pile of back issues of quilting magazines which I've read and reread, often thumbing through them for ideas and never failing to be inspired to make something new.

"I have been clearing out my cupboards and I have some old quilting magazines that I was going to throw out. Are you interested in having them?"

Without a moment's hesitation I replied, "Don't throw them out. I'd love to have them. I still have the ones you gave me before and I use them often. I'll come round for them as soon as I can." In offering me these magazines, Ruby was giving me a treasure trove of ideas, patterns, how-tos and much more.

I came home from Ruby's with several years' worth of back issues. As I quickly glanced through the pile I saw there were only one or two I already had and I could easily pass these extra copies on to a friend who has recently taken up quilting herself.

One of the magazines had a bulge in the middle and I thought I'd better check it out to see if it was something that should be returned to Ruby. I laughed to myself as the pages fell open to reveal the picture and pattern of a baby quilt I had made many years before. Along with it were pattern pieces Ruby had used and, like the thrifty person she is, saved for a future date. This quilt, like most, had a story.

Years ago, I was looking for a pattern to make a quilt for a baby soon to arrive in the family. Time was running out, if the quilt were to be done in time and I had not yet decided on a pattern. Then, while paging through a recently purchased magazine, I saw a picture of a quilt that really appealed to me. Called *Fun Time Bears* it was designed by Theresa Eisinger and featured nine teddy bears sitting, each in its own block, in various poses and with different details added for each teddy. The blocks were bordered with simple sashing and finished with a coordinating border and binding. Apart from the teddies themselves, the quilt was easy to make. But there was no pattern in that issue, just a small picture.

After studying it for some time, I decided that the teddies were not all that difficult to make. Heads, legs and bodies were the same for each block. Arms too, were also the same, just arranged slightly differently for each bear. The extra work would come with the finishing details, and I decided to simplify those by just giving each bear a bow tie to coordinate with the fabrics used in the bodies. No dimensions were available. I would just have to decide on my own. It would be a challenge to draft the pattern from the photo, but one I was sure I could handle. So I began.

The quilt was fun to make, and in due course it was wrapped up and went on its way in time for the new baby's arrival.

About a week after I had sent it, a neighbor dropped by.

"Someone gave me a quilting magazine that I thought you might like to have." Gratefully, I thanked her and after she had left sat down and opened the magazine to enjoy its contents. To my great surprise, there was the full pattern for the teddy bear quilt I had recently worked so hard to finish.

And that was the reason for my smile, for the pattern I was looking at in one of Ruby's back issues was the same pattern I received too late to use.

Now I not only have the printed pattern, but also all the pattern pieces cut out and ready to use. I guess I'll just have to make another teddy bear quilt. There's bound to be a baby who can use it. And this time, I'll do it the easy way.

In Search of Inspiration

$\mathcal{O}$ver the years, our quilters' guild has hosted many gifted quilters who have given interesting talks, brought along samples or shown slides of their beautiful work. They have offered, in their lectures and workshops, many practical suggestions for improving our own quilts.

Part of our guild's aim is to broaden our knowledge of quilting techniques, to develop our individual abilities, to entertain and to inspire us to greater heights of quilting glory. But I'm not sure the guild realizes the other effects these wonderful quilters sometimes have on Mrs. A. (for average) Quilter.

There was the quilt artist who lived in the Pacific Northwest overlooking the ocean. Her quilts were inspired by the world around her and featured the beautiful scenery—trees and flowers, birds and animals, mountains and ocean—visible from her windows. Having graduated from art school, she had begun quilting using traditional techniques and patterns, but had advanced rapidly from that point to become an outstanding fabric artist. Quilter is too limited a term to use for this gifted lady. The slides she showed us of her beautiful quilted works of art could only leave most of us shaking our heads in wonderment and awe at her abilities.

Mrs. A.Q. was equally impressed by a guest who was practical, funny and a good quilter. Her focus was use of fabric,pattern and color. The fact that she owned her own fabric store gave her the opportunity to select up-to-date fabrics for her quilts. She brought many samples of her work with her to illustrate the pointers she wished to share. Although some of them were not yet finished, it didn't matter, for she was so entertaining and so full of good ideas that Mrs. A.Q. along with many others, was almost overwhelmed. Cameras flashed as her quilts were paraded around the auditorium, for no one wanted to forget the ideas she had seen. Mrs. A.Q. bought her book and fully intended to put it to good use in the future.

Another wonderful artist/quilter, as she shared slides of her work, told us about her life and how her quilts were expressions of her interests over the years. We saw quilts, simple in their construction, yet forceful in their original designs, expressing poignant messages about the environment, world peace, women's rights and the various other concerns and causes espoused by this talented woman. Who wouldn't want her quilts to convey such important messages?

But alas for Mrs. A. Quilter. As she left each event, her ego trailed sadly after her. Never in a million years would she be able to accomplish anything nearly as striking, original, thought-provoking or outstanding. The most she could hope for was to be able to get her points all pointy and her appliquéd edges smooth. Was it worth all the effort, her battered ego asked, to continue making such mediocre quilts? Those wonderful quilters inhabited a faraway world she could never hope to enter, much less belong to. They had been interesting, entertaining, awesome in their talents, certainly. But was she inspired to greater heights of personal achievement? Not exactly.

There was another guild meeting that she also remembers well. What the program was that night, she doesn't remember, but there was a show and tell time and she had timidly brought along a quilt she'd been working on for months. Now that it was finished, she wanted to show it to her sister quilters.

After show and tell, several people took the time to tell her how much they admired her quilt. She felt good. Maybe she would keep on quilting. Let's see, there was a scrap quilt pattern she had been thinking about doing. Perhaps she should start on that next.

These kind ladies had provided the ingredient missing in all the lectures and shows. The one thing that really motivates a person. Praise—the ultimate inspirer.

Precisely!

"*P*recision, precision, precision! Those are the first three rules of quilting."

Although it has been over 25 years since I took my first quilting course, I remember those words of my instructor as if they were spoken yesterday. I was an inexperienced novice at the time, determined to do the best work possible. After all, I had some sewing experience and I felt that should be a big bonus. Choosing a sharp pencil and being as accurate as I could, I drew the patterns for my templates. (Could there ever have been a time when the rotary cutter didn't exist?) Carefully I cut my fabric along the painstakingly traced pencil lines with my scissors. So far so good.

Next came the quarter-inch seams. Precise? Well, not exactly. But, hey! I was just a beginner. No one expects perfection from a beginner. I would, no doubt, improve as I gained more experience.

The years have gone by. I've gained lots of experience. I cut with complete accuracy; all my corners meet perfectly; my seams are exactly one-quarter inch all the way along and my quilting is uniformly precise, right? Well, not exactly. In spite of my best efforts, in spite of the quarter-inch foot on my sewing machine, in spite of years of hand quilting, I have yet to reach the heights of precision I envisioned in that first quilting class. Although I can see considerable improvement in some areas, I've come to the conclusion that there must be a gene responsible for the ability to do precise work.

On reflection, I should have known this immediately. For in my previous incarnation as a schoolteacher, I learned early that some children are naturally inclined to be neat and accurate about their work and themselves, and others—the vast majority—leave lots of room for improvement.

The kids with neatness genes were the ones who hung their coats up on the proper hook and arranged their overshoes tidily below them. They colored inside the lines (in those days considered a virtue) without having to be reminded. The pages of their scribblers (if you don't know what they are, ask your grandmother) were invariably clean, with no signs of erasures. They learned to print legibly with little effort and when the time came for them to begin cursive writing, their loops and curves flowed effortlessly from the pencils they always had on hand, points sharpened.

At the other end of the spectrum were the kids who were one continual organizational disaster. They never seemed able to find a pencil and what they did with it when they had one defies description. They were the despair of the less hardened teachers and referred to as a challenge by those with more intestinal fortitude.

It was not surprising, therefore, to find representatives of the complete spectrum in a beginner's quilting class which I agreed to teach for a group of women friends. After a few lessons on basic techniques, the women set about making their own quilting projects. It was with a sense of déjà vu that I left the class one evening. I knew which woman had, as a child, hung her coat up on the proper hook, kept her writing book neat and clean and colored inside the lines. She was the one who cut her strips accurately the first time; whose seams were one-quarter inch all the way and who was halfway though her project when some on the other end of the scale were still trying to cut their fabric right. She was undoubtedly born with the special gene.

Although I have always admired and, yes, envied, such women, I have come to the conclusion that, no matter how much I practice, I'll never be like them. However, as every good teacher knows, not all students can be at the top of the class, but all students can improve.

So, if you, like me, were born without neatness genes take heart.

Yes, you can improve.

No, you may never be perfect.

But, does it really matter?

Precisely!

Fashion Statements

$\mathcal{W}$hat do you wear to a large international quilt festival, such as the one I was planning to attend in Houston, Texas? That question occupied my mind as I pulled out the suitcase in preparation for the trip. Would my few simple attempts at incorporating quilting into the somewhat limited "world of fashion" that is my clothes closet be appropriate? They've been around quite a while—mostly because some of them I would only wear to a quilting event. And any skilful quilter with even one good eye could easily spot the sewing deficiencies. Pack them or not?

I needn't have agonized over this question for one second. For at this event, anything even remotely connected with quilting goes. Women were wearing all kinds of garments that clearly said, "I love quilting." Every conceivable technique—and some that seemed almost inconceivable—were used to embellish all types of clothing, ranging from high fashion items to some that could only be described as "for quilt events only."

Hats were adorned with pins and buttons collected at other quilt shows or traded between owners. Collars were pieced, quilted, embroidered and embellished. Blouses, jackets and skirts featured appliqué, beadwork, hand and machine quilting and pieced designs of all kinds.

And the vests! Pieced, patched, embroidered, cut-worked and beribboned. From A (appliqué) to Y (yo-yos) the whole alphabet of quilting techniques was on display. There were even socks with quilting designs for sale at the show. Yes, socks! From head to toe, quilting was *the* fashion statement of the week.

Their owners may not have been aware of it, but many of these garments, were making their own silent statements. For example, I clearly heard a cluster of colorful Dresden Plate collars say, "Everyone in this quilting group has one of us; but, of course, they only wear us to quilting events."

And as the Seminole pieced and zippered jacket walked by, it called out, "If you only knew how many hours it took her to make me, you'd be amazed."

An elegant, silk, blazer-style jacket with elaborate white work quilting, discreetly murmured, "I belong to a master quilter," while a well-worn, appliquéd, denim shirt smiled smugly, "I'm clearly her favorite."

"I know I don't look great on her, but she put so much work into me, she's determined to wear me anyway," embarrassedly muttered a crazy-quilt skirt on a rather large woman. Nearby, a group of red and white vests sporting red maple leaf motifs stated proudly, "Yes, we're Canadian!"

Finally, amid all the female attire, a man's patchwork leather vest sauntered by and announced, "His wife made me for him and suggested he wear me. He rather likes me, I think."

In all this diversity of fashion, there was one constant—the shoes. Everyone was wearing her most comfortable pair—sandals, runners, walking shoes, or slip-ons, but no high heels anywhere. And so far, no one had figured out a way to incorporate quilting into them. But it wouldn't surprise me if it happens before long. Quilters are an ingenious lot!

Watch Those Whims!

For as long as I can remember, there has been a picture of a cow called Elsie on a well-known brand of milk. How I forgot this, I do not know, but you need to know it before you read on.

$\mathcal{I}$ hadn't seen my friend for nearly 30 years.

Although our families had been close when our children were toddlers, life had taken us in different directions and we had settled about a thousand miles apart. But every Christmas, along with the customary greeting card, we sent each other a letter outlining the highlights of the year that had passed, telling of additions to our families, career changes, new homes and some of the many things that life dealt to us.

So, when the opportunity came to meet again after such a long time, it was with particular pleasure that my husband and I looked forward to spending an evening together with my friend and her husband. After a few minutes of adjustment to the fact that we were nearly 30 years older than when we last met, the intervening years seemed to roll away, and we relaxed and began to enjoy each other's company, as we had so many times in our younger years.

While the meal was cooking on the barbeque, my friend showed me her collection of little wooden houses.

"I love houses," she said, and her delight in her home and her skill at decorating was evident in the beautiful house she was now living in.

We had such a lovely evening together that I decided to show my appreciation of her friendship through the years by making her a miniature wall hanging. Given her love of houses, the little schoolhouse pattern was the obvious choice, and I would use colors that complemented her decor.

Back at home I chose the fabrics carefully and began to plan the piece. There would be four house blocks arranged in a vertical row to make a long narrow hanging, with a tree beside each house for extra interest. Happily cutting and stitching, I thought of my friend's pleasure when she saw the finished piece.

As I assembled the blocks, I was pleased. The colors were right and the blocks looked good on their soft gray-green background, but something was still missing: a focal point or accent of some kind to bring it to life. So, on a whim, from a piece of farmyard print I cut out a little cow and appliquéd it onto the bottom block. It looked as if it were coming around the corner of the house. "That's it!" I thought. Just the touch of whimsy it needed.

It was another two years before I saw my friend again and in the intervening time I hung the miniature on the wall of my sewing room. I wanted to give her the gift in person. Many times as I glanced at the piece, I smiled to myself at the sight of the cow peeking around the corner.

At last, there was another opportunity for us to meet. I carefully packed the little quilt in my suitcase and asked my husband not to let me forget to take it when we went to visit our friends again.

After the greetings were over, I offered my gift to my friend.

"It's lovely," she said. "And look, there's Elsie the cow!"

It was then that the full horror of what I had done, swept over me. That cow, which seemed to be just the right finishing touch, was the one thing I shouldn't have used.

Why? My friend's name was Elsie!

Practice Makes Perfect
(Well, better anyway.)

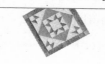

Fit Fabricando Faber. Practice makes perfect. Or, more loosely translated: If your first attempt isn't very good, keep at it and you're sure to improve.

That was the motto of the all-grade school I attended for twelve of the most formative years of my life. Although that was just about the only Latin I learned at school, seeing it on our school crest almost daily for all those years, etched it sharply on my brain. For most of my adult life, it was buried deep in my subconscious and it was only recently that it came to mind in connection with a current quilting effort.

For a number of months I tried to decide on a portable quilt project to take along when traveling. I wanted something that was small and easy to work on. A hand-appliquéd quilt seemed the obvious choice. No sewing machine, rulers, cutting mats or other bulky equipment would be needed once I had made the initial preparations.

After looking through various pattern books, I finally found what I thought would be the ideal project. It was a queen-size quilt with a flower garden pattern. There were five different flowers and five different leaf patterns repeated twelve times, with five extra blocks for the centre, making one hundred and twenty-five appliquéd blocks in all. That would keep me busy for quite a while.

But I hesitated for months before finally investing in the fabric. And the reason for my hesitation dated back many years to my early days as a novice member of our local quilters' guild. At that time, our Standards Committee, who were charged with the responsibility of encouraging high-quality quilting in the guild, offered a mini-workshop on hand appliqué. At the end of the workshop we were offered the opportunity to take home a floral appliqué block to complete, which the committee would critique. Anxious to learn all I could, I eagerly took home a block and worked diligently, and, as I thought, to the best of my ability. I was determined to get "a good mark" for my efforts.

When I had finished I looked critically at my work and I had to admit it wasn't perfect. There were a few bulges where the seam allowances didn't lie quite flat;

and, yes, my leaf points *were* a little knobby (it was hard to get all that seam allowance tucked into such a small space). Turning it over, I could see that my stitches weren't all evenly spaced—but who sees the back of an appliqué anyway? It wouldn't rate a ten or even a nine, I could tell, but maybe an eight, or a seven for sure. So back I went to the next meeting with my block.

The committee members carefully scrutinized each block, after which they made some general comments on how we could all improve, and then handed the blocks back with a slip of paper attached on which they had graded our work. Mercifully, the papers were folded, so only the person who had done the work could see what mark she had been given.

When no one was looking, I unfolded my paper. Six. Only a six! Why, that was barely more than fifty percent. Surely my work had been better than that! But the keen eyes of those expert quilters had noticed every bump and bulge. They *had* looked at the stitches on the back and seen their uneven path. A six was what I had earned and a six was what I deserved. Taking my block and my bruised ego, I slipped away after the meeting and it was a long time before I tried any hand appliqué again. I just wasn't very good at it. Or so I thought.

But the floral quilt pattern looked so pretty and the project was ideal for my purposes. With the sense of picking up a gauntlet thrown down as a challenge many years before, I purchased the necessary fabrics and set to work.

It was then that my old school motto came to mind. *Fit Fabricando Faber.* Practice makes perfect.

After I had completed the first ten blocks I decided to compare them. Yes. The motto was right. The last blocks I had done were definitely an improvement over the first ones. Points were sharper, seams lay flatter, curves were smoother. Not yet perfect, mind you, but better. My old school would be proud of me!

Now, let's see. One hundred and twenty-five blocks … ten finished … only one hundred and fifteen more to go. *Fit Fabricando Faber. Fit Fabricando Faber. Fit Fabricando …*

Housekeeping
for Quilters 101

*H*ousekeeping has never been a great passion of mine and as I grow older, I tackle it with less enthusiasm than ever. I come by this defect, if such it is, honestly. My mother could clean a house with the best of women, but never felt she had to prove it every day. I am also aided and abetted in this weakness by a husband with a very easy-going attitude to cleaning house. He is one who often regards my attempts to keep things clean and in order as excessive and unnecessary, especially if they involve him. When he notices the dust on the bedroom bureaus, I know I've really let things go.

And since I became an enthusiastic quilter things have gotten even worse. I begrudge every minute given to housework that I could be quilting. Time spent washing the floor is time I could be cutting fabric; instead of cleaning cupboards I could be sewing on borders; and as every quilter knows, vacuuming is a waste of time because the floor will soon be littered with threads and fabric scraps again anyway.

However, there is a certain level of untidiness and general disorder below which I am ashamed to sink, so I've devised certain strategies that allow the minimum time for housework and the maximum time for quilting.

Thinking that perhaps there are other dedicated quilters with a similar mind set, I have designed a short course explaining these hard-learned strategies in the hope that they, too, will have more time to indulge their passion. So here it is.

Lesson One: *Getting organized*
Everyone, especially a quilter, realizes the importance of being well organized. Here are ways you can simplify the process.

- Make a list of what has to be done. This does not take very long, but don't be in a hurry to complete it. In fact you can stretch it out for a week or more without devoting more than a couple of minutes a day to actually writing the list. This gives you a great sense of accomplishment and organization without actually spending valuable quilting time doing anything.
- Prioritize your list. At the top of my list would be buying groceries. One has to eat, after all,

and if you have a family to feed this undoubtedly must be done. Something like cleaning the silver would be at the bottom of my list, if it made it at all. Unless, of course, I am expecting the sort of company that I want to impress, such as the Queen, which luckily rarely (in the case of the Queen, never) happens. If my friends aren't already impressed, it's too late to start. But should the Queen decide to visit, cleaning the silver would quickly jump to the top of the list, right after redecorating the house and buying a new outfit.

◆ Have a daily schedule so that by doing a little each day, you can clean your whole house in a week. I'm not talking spring cleaning here—just the places you can usually see. By having a schedule, I have discovered that I can miss a whole week of housework and be all caught up again the next Monday.

Lesson Two: *Cooking*

As already noted above, everyone must eat, even quilters. After the food has been purchased there is still the time-consuming job of cooking. The following practical suggestions will cut down on the time it takes you to put food on the table, which in turn gives you more time to cut up that new fabric you bought.

- When you cook, cook lots of food, so you have lots of leftovers. I have sewed happily many an afternoon, knowing that plunkit was on the menu for dinner. (Plunkit is any leftover dish. You take it out of the fridge, heat it in the microwave and plunkit on the table.)

- Encourage your children to cook. You can't start too early with this. As soon as your little one can spread peanut butter on bread, or stir the jelly, be lavish with your praise. "Billy makes *wonderful* peanut butter sandwiches." "Sally made the jelly dessert *all by herself.*" With any luck, Billy and Sally will grow up to enjoy cooking, thus relieving you of one of the most time consuming aspects of keeping house.

- Encourage your husband likewise, by giving him gifts of cookbooks, kitchen aprons, oven mitts, etcetera. Plan lots of barbecues, where men seem naturally to take charge. Frequent words of praise here pay big dividends also.

- A novice quilter may think that eating out is a good strategy; but not so. By the time it takes to get to where you want to eat, order the meal, eat it, pay the bill and drive home, you could have another quilt well underway. Of course, ordering in is another thing altogether.

Lesson Three: *Cleaning*

Cleaning can be time-consuming, or not, depending on your attitude toward it. I favor the relaxed approach myself, as the following suggestions indicate.

- Prevent dust bunnies in the bedroom by storing all those quilt batts and fabric you bought on sale in containers under the bed. Ignore all other dust as long as possible. Consider it part of the decor.

- Never feel obliged to put your children's toys in order. The absolute futility of this came to me one day when my daughter was a little girl. At one stage she had a passion for undressing all her dolls. (She used to undress herself down to the diaper, too, when in the mood, but happily has grown out of that and diapers.) As I tidied away her toys, I realized I was putting clothes back on her bare dolls! Coming to my senses, I threw toys, naked dolls and doll clothes in the cardboard carton that was her toy box, pushed it into the cupboard and closed the door. If she wanted to undress them, she would have to learn to dress them first!

• Make clean-up time a fun game. For example, "Who can get their rooms tidied up before Mommy sews two more quilt blocks?"

Lesson Four: *Laundry*

The necessity of doing laundry is a fact of life that cannot be ignored, even by the most passionate quilter. The following tips may make this easier to deal with.

• Never, ever, buy clothes that have to be ironed. Remember, next to a rotary cutter, permanent press is the quilter's best friend. Experienced quilters know that ironing clothes is an absolute waste of time. All those clothes are going to get wrinkled again within five minutes of being worn. Is it worth the time it takes to look neatly pressed only as far as the door of your car? Or in the case of children as far as the door of their rooms? I think not!

- By the same token, do not buy clothes that have to be taken to and picked up from the dry cleaners. This can be extremely time-consuming, unless you can talk someone else into doing it for you.

- If you are one of those unfortunates who feel compelled to fold the clean towels, break yourself of the habit. Right away! Yes, you can, and this is how you do it. Buy two hampers, one for dirty towels and one for clean. Take the clean towels out of the dryer and throw them straight into the clean towel hamper. What could be easier? Even the children won't mind doing it. Within days you will wonder why you ever folded towels in the first place. And in the time saved you could easily put your quilt blocks together.

Lesson Five: *Dishwashing*

Doing dishes takes up more valuable time. Even with a dishwasher, someone—perhaps you—has to empty it. On days when you are really pressed for time, there is a very simple way to cut down on the number of dishes used. Simply issue each family member a bowl and spoon at breakfast time and tell them that's all the utensils they get for the day. They are responsible for cleaning the utensils (or not) after they eat. You'll be amazed how much time this saves you. You might even get the quilt basted before midnight.

Lesson Six: *Entertaining*
When unexpected guests arrive at your door and you are at a crucial point in your sewing, you have a number of options.

- Get them involved and occupied while you continue to sew. If you can trust them to cut straight, give them all the old fabrics you were going to cut into squares for scrap quilts, and let them go to it. This is guaranteed to increase your stack of squares and shorten the visits of your unexpected guests.

- Go for a walk. That way, your guests will not even see that you haven't cleaned house for the past three weeks.

- Don't answer the door. This is not very nice, especially if they know you are at home, but sometimes desperate situations call for desperate measures. After all, if the binding simply has to be put on the quilt today, you know what your priorities are.

When you are expecting guests, here's what to do.

- Finish sewing the label on the quilt and then pick the newspapers up off the floor, light some scented candles, and turn the lights down low.
- Put on your most glamorous outfit and pop those frozen canapes in the oven.
- As you greet your guests, admire what the ladies are wearing, tell the men they're growing younger looking every day and you'll be an instant candidate for "Hostess of the Year."

And lastly, to complete this course, always remember the quilter's motto: Quilting forever. Housework whenever.

All Tied Up

INSTRUCTIONS
FOR MAKING SOMETHING
OUT OF OLD NECKTIES

*S*tep 1: See pictures in book borrowed from the library of striking quilted articles made from old neckties. Get very excited about making something similar.

Step 2: Begin collecting neckties. Check husband's closet for out-of-date ties. Suggest he might want to get rid of some he never wears. Realize he will never part with enough ties to make anything. The ones you want most are his favorites, even though he never wears them and they have been out of style for at least 15 years. Start visiting garage sales and second-hand shops.

Step 3: (One month later.) Wash and dry all the ties you have collected. Put them in a bag until you have time to take them apart and cut them.

Step 4: (Six months later.) Find unidentifiable bag in bottom of storage closet. Re-discover ties. Go back to the library to get book on making quilted articles from old neckties. Get excited about project. Vow to start as soon as summer holidays are over.

Step 5: (One year later.) Find bag containing ties in box with uninspiring fabric scraps. Decide this time you will definitely begin project. Get tie book out of the library. Decide project could be quite interesting. Begin to take ties apart. Vow to continue as soon as Christmas is over.

Step 6: (Eight months later.) Absolutely decide to get at that tie project. Go to the library for tie book. Sort ties by color. Discover nearly all ties are either blue and brown. Discover there are not enough ties to make any of the interesting projects in the book. Put out call to friends and neighbors for old ties.

Step 7: (Four months later.) Prepare additional ties. Decide you don't need tie book to create a simple log cabin throw. Begin cutting ties into strips. Sew first block. Discover when the block doesn't turn out square that tie fabric presents new and unforeseen challenges. Go on extended trip.

Step 8: (Later that year.) Return with fresh enthusiasm for completing tie blocks. Actually complete several more.

Step 9: (Three months later.) Move to new house. Rediscover ties as you unpack the last box of quilting supplies.

Step 10: (Three years later.) Receive a bag of old neckties from a friend, which reminds you that you haven't yet finished your tie project.

Step 11: (To be continued.) Maybe.

Name Change

$\mathscr{I}$ have to change the way I describe myself.

You see, I used to think of myself as "Mrs. Average Quilter." For although I have been making quilts for years, I felt I knew my limitations. I'm not a raw beginner. My stitches are a reasonable (in my opinion) size and more or less even, but are far from the beautiful work done by more skillful needlewomen. I own a modest stash of fabric, though never quite enough for the next project, and always have several projects in various stages of incompletion. I enjoy learning new techniques, and have actually completed a few not-too-bad quilts, but nothing I would want to enter in a major quilt show. Just an average quilter. Or so I thought, until I took a class shortly after the release of the results of a survey of American quilters. This survey profiled the average quilt-maker in America and here, in part, is what it discovered and how I fit the profile.

- *Ninety-nine percent of quilters are women. Over 70 percent responded to the questionnaire.* One out of two. I'm a woman.
- *The average quilter is 55 years of age and college educated.* One out of two here and you can guess which one if you want.
- *Her household income is about $75,000.* Not mine, but now I know who buys all those high-priced, hand-painted fabrics.
- *She started 14.2 quilting projects in the last twelve months.* (No figures on how many she finished!) I'm way behind on this one.
- *Her stash of fabrics is valued at about $2,400.* Mine is nowhere near this, but it is some consolation that, with the continuous rise in fabric prices, my little stash is increasing in value every day.
- *She bought 96.5 yards of fabric specifically for quilting.* (No wonder she started so many different projects.) *And if all the fabric bought by U.S. quilters in one year were placed end to end, it would circle the earth two and a quarter times.* (Add Canada, and we'd make it three, easily.) I'm a wee bit short of that amount, even adding old shirts, thrift store and garage sale finds.

Well, as I said above, if you're still with me, I took a class shortly after the results of this survey were released. At the start of the first session the instructor asked us to give our name, tell where we were from and anything else we would like to add about our quilting experience or interests. That's easy, I thought, I'm just an average quilter. So when my turn came (right after the fabric designer and the graphic arts teacher!) I gave my name and hometown and added, "I like to call myself 'Mrs. Average Quilter.'"

"Oh," said the instructor brightly, "you must be one of the women who helped to buy all that fabric which circled the world."

Modestly, I smiled and said no more.

But that's when I decided I had to change my description of myself. "Mrs. Average Quilter" would no longer do. But what term could I use? Somehow "Less than Average" or "Below Average" didn't have much appeal, although they might be more accurate. I pondered long and hard. Well, at least five minutes. And then it came to me.

From now on I'll be "Ada K. Moyles, Not Your Average Quilter." That, at least, should keep people guessing.

Mini-Madness

$\mathscr{I}$ suppose if I had considered a while, I would have realized that the idea that seemed so brilliant when I first thought of it wasn't going to work out. At least, it wasn't going to work out if I was the one who had to make it work.

The idea was simple. I am always interested in trying new patterns. I love the excitement of starting a brand-new project that has sparked my interest. But making big quilts takes time and lots of work. Big quilts also take lots of fabric, which means lots of money. So the more I thought about it, the more it seemed to me that the best way I could satisfy all my quilt-related cravings was to make miniatures.

Miniatures don't take much fabric, I reasoned. They are small and portable and they are done very quickly. I could work on them anywhere—in waiting rooms, in airports, in hotel rooms. I could probably make dozens in no time. I even had visions of taking my little masterpieces along as hostess gifts, where they would, no doubt, be suitably admired and given a place of honor in the hostess' home. Before I had made even one, I was fantasizing about the limitless number of quiltlets I would create and had decided that to aim for a hundred was not an unreasonable number. Not in the first month or two, mind you, but it certainly seemed a possible goal.

Books and magazines further stimulated my imagination and visions of all kinds of miniatures danced in my head.

Where should I start?

With what I already had, seemed the obvious answer.

I had been given a set of heart patterns for paper-piecing. The tiny squares measured only 1¾ inches and each heart had 6 tiny strips plus background. Only small pieces of fabric were required and I knew I could find plenty in my box of scraps. I had lots of pinks, so, with a distinct lack of originality, I decided to make pink hearts on a green background; but I would add interest by increasing the intensity of pink in each of the nine hearts.

I decided to make the first heart the palest pink and the last one the darkest red. For each new heart I would drop the palest of the fabrics used in the previous heart and add a deeper one; then I would reverse the background intensity to have the lightest heart on the darkest green and the darkest heart on the lightest green. It would be a snap. Done by dinnertime!

But, as I said, I should have known myself better.

Calculating the total number of fabrics needed, I came up with 14 pinks and 9 greens, plus borders—24 in all, just for an 8-inch-square quilt!

Choosing the fabric is, for me, the longest and most difficult part of making a quilt, regardless of its size. It took me a whole day just to decide on which pinks and greens to use and the order in which they should occur.

Then came the sewing.

That's when I realized that smaller isn't necessarily quicker. Because I was working with such tiny pieces, I had to be careful to align them exactly right, allowing for the proper angles and including the tiny seam allowance. More than once, a strip was ripped out and carefully realigned or discarded for a new piece. Finally, at the end of day two, the nine heart-blocks were done. (Plus the two extra that had to be discarded because I had sewn the wrong fabrics together.)

Day three saw me adding tiny dark green sashing and a not much bigger border, cutting out the batting and backing. On day four I stitched on the binding. I was finished by dinnertime, all right, but four days later.

Still, I did like the look of my finished mini and decided this was definitely a keeper. The hostess would have to wait for hers. And perhaps 100 miniatures was too optimistic a goal. Maybe 50 would be more realistic.

Bigger projects, in the meantime, had regained their appeal, and it was some time before I began the next miniature. This time I was inspired by an appliqué pattern of a perky little chickadee by Cindy Taylor Clark. It looked so cute sitting on its embroidered branch in its 3½-inch block and it had only five appliqué pieces. It just called out to be made. Four blocks with borders and background sashing would make a nice 12½-inch square. I just had to try it.

Choosing the fabric for this pattern was easy, but the tiny appliquéd pieces were another matter. Appliqué has never been my strong point and those little chickadees had their caps off and on so many times it's a wonder they didn't catch cold! But I finished it. True, it was no master-piece, but I now had miniature two.

I don't know if it is because I am a slow learner or just plain stubborn, but these two experiences still didn't deter me totally from my goal, just reduced it a little. Perhaps 20 miniatures over a longer period would satisfy the quiltlet craving.

A photograph of an exquisitely finished, simple, 9½-inch square, red and green floral wreath on a snowy white background, designed by Diane Lane, caught my attention about the time I received an invitation to a dear friend's fiftieth birthday luncheon. My friend has always been so interested in my quilting that I thought a tiny quilt would be an ideal gift to mark the occasion. To make a long story short, I once again optimistically got to work and, yes, I finished the mini, but long after my friend's birthday had passed. I considered it as a possible Christmas gift, but to my critical eye, it was nowhere near the degree of excellence I had anticipated when I began the simple little square. Like so many other of my projects, I thought it was not good enough to give away, but too good to throw away. So I added it to the other rejects on what I euphemistically call the practice wall in my sewing room.

As I thought back on these less than successful attempts, I had a sense of déjà vu. When my daughters were small, I once tried to make Barbie doll clothes to put in their Christmas stockings. I experienced then the same frustration working with little pieces of fabric as I did with the miniatures.

Like I said, I should have realized that miniatures weren't my thing. But having said that, I am sure that some time in the future another simple little project will catch my eye and I'll try again. Who knows? If I live long enough, I might make that hundred yet. Or even a dozen. But don't place any bets on it.

Buying Time

$\mathcal{O}$ne of the comic strips I most enjoy reading is *Pickles*, drawn by Brian Crane. In my all-time favorite strip, Earl is sitting on a bench with his buddy pondering the meaning of life. His buddy asks, "Have you ever thought about the concept of eternity? You know, how it goes on and on."

"Yeah, I have," replies Earl. "It's usually when I'm at the fabric store with my wife."

I chuckled aloud when my husband showed me this strip. I knew he identified with it. But I also smiled for another reason I have the same experience when in a hardware store with my husband. Which just goes to show there is another little-recognized difference between men and women. When a man is in a fabric shop, it feels like an eternity. When a woman is in a fabric shop, time stands still.

The majority of quilters that I know regard the buying of fabric as something that takes time and involves weighty decisions regarding patterns and colors, border prints vs. piecing, being thrifty vs. throwing caution to the winds and buying the expensive fabrics they really want.

Shopping for fabric, as practised by the dedicated quilter, is a real art. It reaches its highest form when the quilter is in a new town or city and is making a tour of the quilt shops there. More than likely, she has some idea of what her next project might be and, of course, the fabric she needs is not available in her own home town. She needs an excuse after all, especially if she is traveling with her spouse. However, she is not confining herself to this one project, but is leaving her options open, just in case a more appealing pattern presents itself.

Even before our quilter enters the quilt store, she is eagerly anticipating what she might find. She may have heard from other quilters about the store, or have seen it advertised. Such phrases as "a quilter's dream," "everything a quilter needs," "miles of fabric," "thousands of bolts" have effectively done their work and she is preconditioned to expect to find not only what she thinks she wants, but much more than she could ever have imagined.

Once inside, her eyes are drawn to the beautiful quilts skilfully displayed all around the store. Pinned to each one are the details of the classes in which she, too, can make any one (or all) of these quilts. And of course all the fabrics are available in the store. If Mrs. A.Q. can resist the temptation to sign up for one of the courses (this is made easy only if she is leaving town the next day and her airline tickets cannot be changed), her next move will be to make a tour of the quilt shop.

Aisle by aisle, she circulates through the store, examining rows of fabric bolts, pulling out one here and one there for a better look at the pattern, or to more carefully check the color.

In between the fabrics are racks of patterns. These must be given at least a cursory examination. Is there something here to put aside for future use? Magazine and book stands also deserve her attention. Who knows what treasures she might find? Then there are the threads, gadgets and other notions. No quilter ever has enough different colors and types of thread, and new gadgets are almost irresistible, even though very few quilters have actually used all the gadgets they already have.

Finally, the rumbling of her stomach, telling her it's past lunch time, motivates her to begin making her selections. Back and forth from shelves to counter she goes. A pile of bolts accumulates on the cutting table, as visions of the wonderful quilts she will be making flit through her mind. When she can no longer see over the top and bolts start sliding onto the floor, she decides she had better narrow down her choices. This is the hard part.

Each fabric has spoken to her.

There are the children's fabrics, perfect to add to the "I spy" blocks she has been accumulating. There are land-scapes—just the thing for the outdoor scene in the wall-hanging pattern she bought at the last store. There are border prints that might be useful in the queen-size quilt she fully intends to start soon. And how can she not buy those soft, cuddly flannels? They would be ideal for the baby quilts waiting to be made. Of course the sale tables have not been overlooked. Some of those fabrics would be just fine for backings and what a bargain!

While her choices are being measured and cut, she experiences a sense of euphoria. In her mind she already envisions the finished quilts. She hands over her credit card with hardly a glance at the total on the cash register. What fun she will have using all these fabrics.

As she leaves the shop, she can hardly wait to get started.

"What took you so long?" her spouse asks.

"I wasn't very long, was I? It didn't seem long to me."

Serendipity-doodah!

*Serendipity: the faculty of making happy
and unexpected discoveries by accident.*

Chocolate lovers get it from an unusually delicious,
freshly baked, lavishly iced brownie; coffee lovers get it
from the freshly brewed, early morning cup that jump-
starts their day. But for quilters it sometimes comes
from the most unexpected sources and in the most
unexpected circumstances.

I'm talking about the glow of delight and pleasure
that occurs when you make a happy and unexpected
discovery that lights up your world. Such a serendipitous
occurrence was mine while attending the wonderful quilt
festival in Houston. And it came not from the marvelous
displays of breathtakingly beautiful quilts, or from the
joys of meeting and mixing with quilters from all over
the world, or from the all-day workshop I attended, but
unexpectedly, at the tail-end of a morning session from
which I had not expected anything exceptional.

This is how it happened.

My daughter and I were attending a sampler class, where 40 different teachers simultaneously demonstrated their particular interests, areas of expertise or new ideas in 15- or 20-minute segments, which were repeated continuously throughout the two-hour session. We had been moving slowly, along with hundreds of others, from table to table and had seen many novel ideas displayed and demonstrated, collected useful hints for improving our quilting and generally had a satisfying morning. With only 20 minutes left we were working our way out of the large room where the session was held, when we were attracted by an intriguing display of unusual wall hangings with the caption "Simple blocks. Stunning quilts." That sounds like my style of quilting, especially the "simple blocks" bit, I thought; and don't we all want to make stunning quilts? We paused to listen.

The instructor, Eileen Sullivan, was just about at the end of her demonstration, but seeing the interest of ourselves and others agreed to repeat it one more time. In the few minutes remaining, Eileen showed us how to design our own blocks for use with foundation piecing on freezer-paper, in a no-template method. She clearly outlined the steps required and illustrated the procedure with pictures and samples, supplemented by a descriptive handout sheet.

By the time she had finished, I was hooked! This was some-thing I wanted to try immediately! I couldn't wait to get started.

But then a little inner voice spoke up. Remember, it cautioned, you decided that before you began any new project, it had to pass three tests:

1. Do I have the time to do it?
2. Is it affordable?
3. Do I have a use for it?

You are right, of course, I said to the voice. I'll apply the tests.

Test number one was easy. I was staying with my daughter for a few days after the festival with only a long-term hand-appliqué project to work on. Of course, I had no quilting tools with me, but my daughter, a beginning quilter, already had the basic tools *and* a new sewing machine that I was longing for an excuse to try out.

Test two? Well, the ideas could be used in a small project less than 32 inches square, so the cost was affordable.

Three? That was more difficult, but with two out of three in favor, it was almost a sure go.

What finally cast the deciding vote was a serendipitous visit to a fabric store that afternoon. As we looked around at all the lovely displays and bolts of beautiful fabric, a bundle of six fat quarters in Christmas colors of red, green, gold and cream caught my eye. That was it! The answer to question three. I could use the finished item as a Christmas table-topper. I paid for the fabric, the die was cast, and I smiled all the way to my daughter's home, eager to begin.

Barely had the last crumbs of a hastily prepared sandwich been swallowed before we had pencils in hand and were sketching possible block designs. Very soon, I had decided on the block pattern and was busily making my freezer-paper foundations. By the time the afternoon was over I was ready to make a sample six-inch block. I was intrigued with each step of the procedure and thoroughly enjoying myself.

Then came the crunch. With only 6 fat quarters and 10 pieces in each block, I knew I would have to use some fabrics more than once. For the largest piece I decided to use a boldly striped cotton, positioning it in the same way in each of the 16 blocks. Would I have enough? It would be a tight squeeze. But (more serendipity) with hardly a thread to spare, I cut out the last piece.

Before long, all 16 blocks were ready to be positioned. This was the fun part, as up until this stage, I really had no idea how the finished quilt was going to look. My daughter and I laid out the blocks in a square and stood back for the full effect. Then we arranged, rearranged and looked again. Eileen had said it was a good idea to photograph the various arrangements and look at the photographs before deciding on the final placement of the blocks. So I dutifully got out my camera, knowing full well that, as I was having such a good time, I would have this quilt finished before I got the film developed. And I did.

As I viewed the various block arrangements, the reds in one placement seemed to produce a design vaguely reminiscent of poinsettias. It was an obvious choice for a Christmas quilt. By the time I boarded the airplane on my way back home, the blocks were in my suitcase, neatly sewn together, awaiting the borders and backing, which I knew I could make from some fabric in my home stash. This done, the few remaining scraps of the original fabrics were combined with matching fabrics to make the binding.

All that was left was the quilting. And (more serendipity) it was the perfect project to try out another idea I had learned at the festival. With a gold metallic thread in the machine bobbin, I machine quilted in long straight lines on the back of the quilt. The resulting sparkle enhanced the Christmas fabric on the front of the quilt and I was pleased with the result. So pleased, in fact, and so delighted with the simplicity and ease of the whole process that I decided it would be an appropriate quilt to take to our Guild's pre-Christmas show and tell.

It was well-received and the interest it aroused was very gratifying. So much so that I'm thinking of teaching a workshop for those who want to learn how to make this project. And I hope that for them it will be, as it was for me, serendipity all the way!

I'm Alright, Jack!

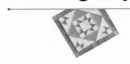

$\mathcal{W}$e had just had a very pleasant visit with our neighbor, Jack, and were saying our goodbyes, when the warning bells went off. No, not the fire alarm, but those inner promptings that make you take a second look at what you are doing, saying, or thinking about.

Jack is a talented craftsman whose medium is stained glass. We had been admiring his latest creations and he had been describing how he worked. It sounded very familiar to me, as there are many similarities between stained glass work and quilting. We both start with large pieces of material, cut them up into smaller pieces and, with considerable time and effort, put them back together again, to produce both useful and beautiful works of art. Quilters have often attempted to imitate the stained glass look in their quilts and stained glass artists have been known to use quilt patterns as well. In the Museum of the American Quilter's Society in Paducah, Kentucky, both arts are combined in their beautiful stained glass quilt-patterned windows.

So I was very interested in hearing about Jack's retirement hobby.

He had been telling us that once he gets a new idea or a request for another piece, he has to get right to work on it. "I can't wait to get started. It's like an obsession," he said.

"Oh, I know all about obsessions," my husband observed, with a knowing look in my direction. "My wife's an obsessive quilter."

Me? Obsessive? Just a minute now. That's going a bit far, isn't it? Yes, quilting is my favorite pastime. I do spend many hours at it. I eagerly begin new projects. But does that make me obsessive? I'll admit to being captivated by quilting, even passionate, but obsessive? No. That's definitely going too far.

Obsessive is Jack Nicholson in *As Good As It Gets* carefully avoiding the cracks in the sidewalks and carrying his own cutlery to restaurants. Such bizarre behavior is definitely obsessive. You wouldn't catch me doing anything so obviously unhealthy as that. Cutting up perfectly good lengths of fabric into little tiny pieces and sewing them back together again is not the same at all.

Nevertheless, a nagging doubt had been planted in my mind. So, having often seen self-diagnostic questionnaires in popular magazines, I thought it might be worthwhile to draw up such a quiz for myself and for other quilters who might have had similar doubts about how quilting might be affecting their mental health.

If you feel anxious on this point, please feel free to use the following questionnaire as a first step in your self-assessment, before you rush off to see an expensive therapist.

CHECK YOUR MENTAL HEALTH
A Questionnaire for Quilters

(For each of the following questions
answer *Never, Sometimes* or *All the Time*.)

1. When you hear the words "baby," "graduation," "wedding" or "anniversary" do you automatically think "quilt"?
2. Do you lie awake in bed at night thinking about the next quilt project or the one you are currently working on?
3. Do you look at fabrics people are wearing with an eye to how they would look in a quilt?

4. Do you study the tiled floors in public places, such as washrooms, to see if the patterns could be used in a quilt?

5. When you visit a new town or city, do you check the yellow pages for quilt/fabric stores and include them on your itinerary?

6. When in a new quilt/fabric store do you buy fabric, patterns or gadgets, even though you have no immediate use for them?

7. Do you store (hide) packages of quilt batting and plastic storage bins full of fabrics under your bed because you have filled up all the other storage areas in your home with other quilt batts and fabrics?

8. Do you sign up for quilt classes, even though you haven't finished all the projects you began in the last ten classes you took?

9. Are you ever late for an event because you just had to finish the quilt piece you were working on?

10. Do you carry photos of your quilts with you wherever you go, in case you meet another quilter?

For each time you answered *Never* score 0; for each *Sometimes* score 1 point; for each *All the Time* score 2 points. Add your total score.

If your score is 0 you have nothing to worry about, but what do you do with your time? If your score is 1-10 you may have a problem. Keep monitoring the situation. If your score is over 10, although you may think this is cause for concern, relax. You aren't obsessive at all.

How do I know this?

According to my dictionary an obsession is "an unreasonably persistent idea in the mind." And there is nothing unreasonable about your ob—— *interest* in quilting. Ask any quilter. As they will attest, you (and I) are perfectly normal quilters acting in perfectly normal ways.

Whew! That's a relief.

Excuse me now, but I have to go and cut up some more fabric.

A Veritable Feast

$\mathscr{I}$ went to a banquet the other evening and I came away full. Very full, indeed.

It was really the regular meeting of our local quilters' guild, and although we end our year with an annual sit-down banquet in June, this mid-winter meeting was truly a feast of delight. The menu was fairly standard—appetizers, salad, main course, dessert, coffee. The quality was outstanding and the amounts served prodigious. Let me describe it for you.

First there were the appetizers. Upon entering the meeting place, the foyer was filled with tables containing a wide assortment of goodies to pique a quilter's palate. Projects small and large were set out for delectation and possible participation: charity projects for the local hospitals, quilt work for Habitat for Humanity houses, a charm square exchange, sign-up sheets for quilting weekends and workshops, the monthly book draw and the library books available for guild members to borrow.

Following the appetizers came the salad course. The show-and-tell display covered the two side sections of the auditorium where the guild meets. The variety of colors, patterns, techniques and ideas presented in the projects brought for display were not only a treat for the quilter's palate, but offered lots of useful ideas for future projects.

Then the main course was served. Not many banquets feature a main course of leftovers, but that was what was on the menu that night. A lively, entertaining quilter displayed some of the dozens of scrap quilts she had made. As well as giving us design ideas, she gave us numerous hints for organizing our fabric scraps, how to make the most of the sewing time available to us and practical suggestions for using even the smallest scraps of fabric. She's the only quilter I've heard of who saves the "ears" cut off triangles, putting them in a glass jar that she keeps by her sewing machine. Her grandchildren love to make pictures out of these tiny pieces by sprinkling them onto glue-covered cardboard—also scraps, saved from such things as cereal boxes and panty-hose packages.

By this time we were feeling quite full, as you can imagine. So it was a good thing the dessert course was actually that—dessert. At the end of every guild meeting we have a time when we can share friendship and swap quilting stories and ideas with other quilters over some home-baked goodies. We drink our punch or coffee out of our own mugs, brought to the meeting in quilted mug-totes—a small project of several years ago, when the guild became more conscious of the need to eliminate waste in our environment.

At the end of the evening and the banquet, I came away feeling full. Full of admiration for the creative people in our guild, full of new ideas for future projects and full of enthusiasm for quilting in general and our guild in particular.

The Secret Quilt

"*W*ill you make a quilt for me?"

The request came during a phone call from my friend Lorraine, who had been a long-time admirer of my quilts. We had often discussed the possibility that some day she would ask me to make her a quilt and now the time had come.

Lorraine and her husband, Doug, were about to retire after spending their lives in church ministry. Money had never been plentiful, and a handmade quilt was not a necessity, but with retirement on the horizon, Lorraine dearly wished to have a special quilt to grace the bed in their retirement home.

Happy for her and, it must be admitted, happy for myself at the prospect of making a special quilt for a good friend, I readily agreed. We discussed some preliminary ideas and then decided that the best thing would be for us to get together some evening and decide on patterns and colors so the quilt would be just what she wanted.

"I'll discuss it with Doug," Lorraine said, with excitement in her voice, "and let you know when we are free and we can plan from there."

The next phone call came from Doug.

"Lorraine has been telling me that she asked you to make a quilt for her," he began. "I'm not quite sure how to put this, but I have had to tell her that I don't want her to do this right now. You see, our daughter Caroline is making a quilt for her as a surprise retirement gift, and I don't want to spoil it for her. I hope you don't mind?"

Of course, I didn't mind. What could be more special than a quilt made for you by your own daughter? But what could I say to Lorraine?

"Don't worry. I'll think of something and have her phone you. And thank you for being so understanding."

It was a very subdued Lorraine who called the next day. "I'm really sorry, Ada, but for some reason I can't understand, Doug doesn't want me to go ahead with this quilt right now. I don't ask for much and he's usually so understanding. He must have a good reason, but I'm sorry you won't be making me a quilt."

"I'm sorry too," I said. "I was looking forward to doing it, but Doug must have a good reason, as you say. Don't feel bad on my account. I have lots of projects to keep me busy." I was glad that I was speaking on the phone and not face to face, for it was all I could do to be properly sympathetic and not let a tell-tale giggle escape to give a hint that I knew something she didn't.

Nothing more was said, but in the months that followed I often wondered how Caroline's quilt was coming along.

About a month before their official retirement, I was chatting with Lorraine about her future plans and all the decisions moving into a new home entails. I was studiously avoiding any mention of quilts, when she suddenly said, "You know, Ada, I want you to know that Doug told me about the quilt Caroline is making for me. He said he couldn't stand all the deception any longer. Of course, she doesn't know that I know. But I'm really excited and looking forward to seeing it."

We had a good laugh at the memory of the previous conversations and parted with a smile.

On the evening of their retirement dinner, I had the opportunity to meet Caroline and she told me that she knew all about her father's dilemma when her mother asked me to make a quilt. Then she told me about the pleasure she had in selecting colors she thought her mother would like and the special significance of the patterns she had chosen. She could hardly wait for her mother to see it.

No, her mother didn't know about it. It was to going to be a great surprise, she said. She had put it on the bed in her parents' new apartment and her mother would see it the next day. She would send me a photo, if I wished to see it.

Of course I would. That was a very special quilt. Her mother would love it, I was sure. Once again, it was all I could do to keep my voice steady.

A few weeks later, I met Lorraine again. She was overjoyed with her long-awaited quilt. It was lovely. Her daughter had done such a beautiful job on it. The colors were perfect for the room and she was thrilled to have such a special quilt in her new home.

I was almost as happy as Lorraine, knowing that no quilt of mine, however well made, could possibly match the joy her daughter's quilt had given and would continue to give her for years to come.

It was the best quilt I never made.

Leftovers

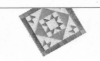

 $\mathscr{T}$ hank goodness for leftovers, I thought, as I hurried to the kitchen to prepare lunch. I had been sewing all morning and it was too late to cook anything fresh, but the remains of a macaroni and cheese casserole from the day before would do just fine for another meal. Fortunately, I am married to a man who is pretty undemanding when it comes to food. And he's especially fond of macaroni and cheese. So leftovers it would be.

Since the children moved out, leftovers have featured frequently on the menu. At first, I found it difficult to downsize from preparing meals for five (and often more) to cooking for just two. But once I realized how easy it was to just reheat previously prepared food, I found myself cooking extra amounts so that I wouldn't have to cook another day. Of course, there is another reason for these planned leftovers. Less time cooking means more time quilting.

Some leftovers have turned into quite remarkable dishes. Of course there are those that elicit the question, "What *is* this?" or the even more unwelcome comment,

"Not this again!" But many a good soup has been made in our household from recycled ingredients, and no one even suspected.

Thank goodness for leftovers, I thought, as I found just the small piece I needed to finish the wall hanging I was working on. Time was at a premium and I wanted to finish this quilt, so the discovery of that bit of fabric left over from another project was just what I needed.

As with food, leftover fabric can be recycled, and made into beautiful quilts. Quilters know that many quilts were originally made from leftover and recycled fabrics. Judging by the number of books that feature these scrap quilts, they are still very popular. Most quilters have a box or bag of leftovers that they plan to turn into a quilt someday.

And the beauty of leftover fabrics, as opposed to leftover foods, is that they don't turn green or fuzzy, if they are left too long unused. Vintage fabrics are still popular and quilters everywhere are recycling jeans, T-shirts, old socks, neckties and almost any fabric you can name into quilts that are used, loved and even treasured by their recipients.

Whether foods or fabrics, the second time around can be as satisfying as the first. So let's hear it for leftovers!

Full Circle

$\mathcal{A}$s soon as I saw the picture of the quilt, I knew I was destined to make it.

It was a striking log cabin pattern, in a barn-raising setting, with bands of golds, reds and greens separated by beige neutrals. A center medallion depicted a log cabin in the wilds of Canada and scattered here and there were individual maple leaf blocks. It was the quintessential Canadian quilt, well within my capabilities and it used colors I loved—all of which gave it an irresistible appeal.

The magazine which featured the quilt pattern also contained an article about the designer, Dianne Jansson, a quilt teacher living in Western Canada. I definitely wanted to make that quilt, but having no immediate reason or use for it, I filed the magazine away for future reference.

From time to time, I would look at the cover photo, just to reassure myself that it was as attractive as I remembered, and, yes, it definitely was.

Nearly two years went by before I found the perfect reason to begin making it.

My husband and I were planning to take a long awaited trip to Australia to visit our son-in-law's parents, Marian and Graeme, and I knew this quilt would be the perfect gift for them. They had visited us in Canada and were quite appreciative of my quilting. Marian's artistic eye, which had given some valuable input on a work-in-progress, and Graeme's enthusiasm were a boost to my creativity.

So I set to work and happily began to collect my fabrics. In my stash were fabrics my daughter had brought from Down Under and others given to me by an extremely generous visitor from Australia. By good fortune, most of the colors were exactly those called for in the pattern. They would add a special touch.

Of course, like many quilters, I never make a quilt exactly as the pattern indicates. Whether it's the color scheme, the quilting pattern, the borders, or the mistakes, every quilt has some little individual changes that make it my very own. So it was with this one.

I decided to replace some of the maple leaves with photos and symbols that would make this a very personal quilt. I included a kangaroo and a koala for Australia, a beaver and a maple leaf for Canada, fabric pictures of Aussie houses in the outback and a photo of a little creek in Canada where our Australian friends had seen beavers at work. Then I added photos of Marian and Graeme, my husband and myself and our daughter and son-in-law.

I knew that they would enjoy owning the quilt as much as I had enjoyed making it.

What I didn't know was how much *I* would appreciate having made it. For, unknown to me, it was to have a far wider audience than I had intended. And this is how it happened.

"Marian has some friends who are quilters, and they would enjoy meeting you," said Graeme, during a phone call, when the visit was in the planning stages.

"That would be nice. I'm sure I would enjoy meeting them, too," I replied innocently, envisioning a group of three or four ladies visiting in Marian's home, talking quilting over a nice cup of tea. All very relaxed, I imagined.

Little did I know how different it would be.

The initial shock came via an email. Would I be willing to take part in a quilting seminar one morning during my visit?

Who? Me? What could I have to say that would possibly interest quilters in my own country, let alone a country I had never even been to? Who would be at this seminar anyway and how many? Australia had lots and lots of expert quilters. What would they already know? Was there *anything* I knew that they didn't? I doubted it. Questions flooded my mind, but not wanting to disappoint my hosts and friends, I considered the request.

Then I remembered that I was bringing the Canadian quilt. I could show the quilt and talk a bit about it and perhaps read a column or two from my "Views from the Attic" series and that would be my contribution to the seminar.

Rather hoping that what I had in mind was not what was wanted, I emailed my ideas back, vaguely suggesting that I could bring a piece of quilting to show and saying I could probably fill about 30 minutes, if that was enough, and asked for more details.

That sounds great, was the sum of Graeme's reply.

So I was committed. Or, I felt, I should have been!

As the time for our departure became imminent, I received another shock.

With an apology for not getting back to me sooner, Graeme informed me that the seminar was now scheduled to take place between 10:30 am and 3:00 pm. The quilters were really excited about my coming and flyers advertising the event were being distributed to the quilt stores in the area. Quilters were being asked to bring their work for display or comment. And I was the entire program!

Immediate panic. Oh, no. What have I gotten myself into? What could I do to fill all that time? Quickly I pieced together some simple blocks that could be used to demonstrate different techniques for the ladies to copy if they wished and hoped that there would be lots and lots of show and tell.

But all that panic was needless. As I should have remembered, quilters are among the nicest people in the world. The ladies who came to that seminar brought beautiful work to display; they listened with interest to what I had to say; they took time to talk with me during the lunch break and after the program ended; they admired my quilt (one lovely woman asked for the pattern—the ultimate compliment) and they even said they learned something new.

To finish the story, Marian and Graeme loved their quilt and it is hanging, prominently displayed, in their home. One last thing: in preparing the talk about the Canadian quilt I went back to the magazine in which it was featured and read once more about the Western Canadian designer. It was then I realized that Dianne Jansson was originally from Australia.

The quilt had come full circle.

The Crowning Touch

$\mathscr{I}$ve been called quite a few names in my time. Most of them, I hasten to add, quite acceptable. I've been "her father's daughter" to those who thought I looked like him, "her mother's daughter" by those who thought I resembled her, "our little sister" by my siblings, "teacher's pet" by some nasty boy in grade three, "wife," "mom," "teacher" and "quilter," to name just a few.

But I've never been called a princess. That is until just recently.

I had agreed to teach a small group of women (no more than eight) how to do hand appliqué at the request of Linda, a good friend who had taken a quilting basics course from me some time ago. She had, as she put it, "been bitten by the quilting bug"and was now organizing quilting classes at our church for other women who wanted to learn the craft.

When I had stipulated "small group" I had no idea how small it would be. Six women signed up for the class, but on the first night only five showed up. One of these, a woman who had made many quilts, admitted she had arthritis and couldn't hold a needle comfortably. She went to help the novice quilters in the piecing class. Another decided that she would rather take the scrap-booking class, being offered at the same time. That was fine with me. It would be easier to give individual attention to the remaining three. On week two, another woman told me she suffered badly from migraines and was afraid bending her head to concentrate on her work might be a trigger. Now there were only three of us: Joy, Sarah and myself.

Joy and Sarah were both friends. Joy was familiar with my work, as she worked on a charity auction committee to which I donated a quilt each year. She had quite a bit of experience in sewing and had recently begun making place-mats, baby quilts and tablerunners. She brought some of her handwork to show us and it was evident that she had a good eye for color and made excellent fabric choices.

Sarah was a novice quilter. I had helped her through the making of her first quilt for a little grandson and she was starting another pieced quilt as a surprise for a daughter. Like Joy, she was interested in learning something new but informed me that she would not be able to attend all of the six or eight lessons I had planned, as she had commitments out of town during that time.

With only two students (and occasionally just one), the classes were easy enough. I was able to bring some of my own work-in-progress and as we each stitched on our own projects we chatted and shared together as women do.

One evening as we were sitting together at the table stitching our blocks, Joy said to me, "I saw a little notepad the other day. It was the kind with a magnet on the back that you put on your fridge. The title was really cute and I thought of you. It said "Princess Quilt-a-Lot." You do more quilting than anyone else I know."

"That's a nice compliment," I laughed as we continued our sewing. "I've never been called a princess before."

The next week as Joy was unpacking her quilting supplies, she handed me a small parcel. "This is for you, Princess Quilt-a-Lot," she said with a smile. I opened it, and there was the notepad with a quilt-style checkered border and the title at the top. I thanked her for it and tucked it into my quilt bag.

Later that evening, as I unpacked the bag, I took another look at the notepad and burst out laughing.

With quilting on our minds, Joy and I had misread the title. What it really said was "Princess of Quite-a-Lot." Not just quilting, mind you, but a lot of other things as well!

I put it on my fridge and as I look at it daily, I reflect on my new title. I never expected to be called a princess, but, hey, if the crown fits ...

Down with False Modesty

"*I* only brought it to encourage other beginning quilters to bring their quilts," said one lady recently at our guild's show and tell. The implication was clear. This wasn't a very good quilt. Not really in the same category as all the rest. It really didn't deserve to be shown.

Now that was a lot of nonsense. It was a perfectly lovely quilt. At our show and tell there are no judges. Everyone's quilt is a minor masterpiece and deserves its moment on stage. Yet, like so many other quilters, this woman clearly suffered from a false sense of modesty, an affliction all too common among quilters.

"It's only a scrap quilt." (Scrap quilts are beautiful, too.)

"I just threw it together." (*We* know how long it takes to make a quilt like that.)

"There are lots of mistakes." (So?)

I've seen and heard it all too often. As quilters we are always striving to improve our work and that is laudable. But it doesn't necessarily follow that what we have just completed isn't deserving of praise or has no merit. Who among us would claim to do perfect work? Yet, we so often wear an air of fake humility. We are humble people with a lot to be humble about, we seem to be saying. But inside, we are feeling quite different.

I must admit I've been guilty of this false modesty myself on occasion.

Hanging in my sewing room are what I call "practice pieces"—those in which I was trying a new technique. Sometimes the results were less than satisfactory and I know that if I did those pieces again, I would do better. And yes, I've been guilty of pointing out the mistakes, or denigrating work that took me hours to complete—and to perfect strangers to quilting, who are full of admiration for everything they see and can't tell appliqué from piecing when it is right before their eyes.

But no more.

From now on my work is going to be shown proudly and I will accept any and all compliments without any negative responses on my part. I will acknowledge only to myself how I really feel about what I've done. (I've spent a lot of hours on this project and it looks pretty good to me. *I* know it's not perfect, but if you can't see the mistakes I'm not going to point them out.)

"But why this about-face?" you ask.

It is all because of Colleen. She came to me for help with her very first quilting project. Nothing simple, like a nine-patch or log cabin. No, she had bought a pattern for a beautiful wall hanging with dozens of tiny pieces to be machine-appliquéd in place, then the whole piece was to be hand-quilted. Not in the least daunted by the challenge facing her, she was eager to get started.

Happy to help a budding quilter, I readily agreed to assist in whatever way I could. Sometimes a "How do I do this?" call came over the phone, and sometimes Colleen brought the work-in-progress to my house and we discussed the next step in the project. Always, Colleen was full of enthusiasm.

"I can't believe I'm doing this."

"This is so much work, but so much fun!"

"Doesn't it look great?"

"My friends will never believe I made this."

After I had been out of town for several weeks, Colleen called to bring me up to date on her work. I could hear the excitement in her voice.

"It's finished and it's absolutely gorgeous. I can't wait to show it to you."

"I can't wait to see it. I'll bet it looks fantastic."

And it does. No sense of false modesty anywhere. And if there are any mistakes, I can't see them. Quilters, take note.

Dream On

$\mathcal{I}$ have a dream.

No, it's not a dream for racial equality, or the eradication of poverty, or world peace, as wonderful as those dreams are and as much as I long for them to become reality.

No. My dream is much less grandiose, much more down-to-earth and, I have to say, much more mundane. And of course, you have already guessed that it has to do with quilting.

My dream is of the ideal quilt studio. I have had this dream for a long while and it was revived recently, when I read several articles about well-known quilt artists who let us see into their quilting studios. Oh, those studios were wonderful! Sewing machines rested on tables adjusted to the height of the individual. No aching backs or sore necks for these quilters.

Fabrics were neatly arranged on shelves, organized according to color and shade. No running out to the nearest fabric shop for that one extra piece needed to put the finishing touch on the last blocks. These quilters had choices at their fingertips.

Large areas of shelving and cupboards held all their quilting supplies; dozens of spools of thread were arranged in purpose-built cabinets or hung on spool racks. Irons and boards were situated conveniently close to the sewing machine; cutting tables, rulers and mats of various shapes and sizes were near at hand. No wonder those quilters were able to produce such beautiful quilts. Yes, I know it takes more than a great studio to produce a great quilt, but I bet every one of those quilt artists would agree that it sure helps.

So my dream of the ideal studio was revived once more.

Now, I hasten to add that I'm not a person who simply dreams and does nothing about it. Over the years I have done my best to make my dream a reality. For years I sewed at the kitchen table, manoeuvring for space with the children's homework, the latest mail, anything that anyone couldn't find another space for and, of course, meals. But when the last of the children left home, I converted a bedroom into a sewing room, the first step in my quest for the ideal studio. When I say *converted* I really mean I just moved my sewing stuff into it and claimed it as my own, but I left the bed, the bureau and the old desk, just in case she might want to come home occasionally. It was just as well I did, for, like many of her generation, she moved out and moved back. So much for my sewing room!

Eventually, she married and moved away and the room was mine again. The furniture stayed. I used the bed for laying out partially completed tops and stored batting and fabric underneath; the desk became my sewing table, even though it was small and I frequently banged my knees on its corners; the bureau held thread, gadgets, fabric and anything else that I could stuff into it. An old table top was set on trestle legs, and while it was too wobbly for a cutting table, it was fine for laying out materials.

As the years passed, I have come a little closer to my dream. A move to a new house gave me an area just for sewing. We bought a new kitchen table and I just happened to have room in my sewing area for the old one, which had served double duty as my cutting table for many years. I gladly exchanged the small bookcase I had been using for a larger one to hold my growing collection of quilting books and magazines. When my husband bought a set of shelves for his workshop, then decided he didn't want them, he generously offered them to me to store my materials. And over the years I have amassed quite a collection of shoe boxes, plastic baskets and bins of all sizes to hold leftover pieces of fabric, unused fat quarters, works-in-progress, works that might be in progress at a future date, and assorted fabrics that I know I will find a use for some day, although I can't, at the moment, think for what.

So, in comparison to where I started, I have made progress.

But the other day I saw my dream studio.

I walked in the door and there it was! Bolt after bolt of fabric was all neatly arranged according to color on purpose-built shelves. Cabinets held spools of thread of all imaginable types, sizes and colors. Racks of quilting magazines and books were neatly displayed so their titles were clearly visible. Around the room, completed quilts adorned the walls, attesting to the expertise of their maker. Tucked in a corner was an antique sewing machine, artistically displayed on an equally antique, quilt-covered table, next to which a comfortable chair invited one to sit and browse through books and magazines while the creative juices flowed; and in a separate area, there were large tables, perfect for cutting, laying out or basting a quilt, with sewing machines set up ready to sew.

I sighed over the perfection of it all. There it was. My ideal studio.

A quilt shop!

Organizational Skills

$\mathcal{I}$t was time to get organized, I told myself sternly, after searching fruitlessly for a piece of fabric I knew I had somewhere. And that was only a day after I had looked in vain in all the places I knew it might be—and in some places I was sure it wouldn't be—for the pattern for a guild charity project I was sure I had brought home. Surveying the assortment of cupboards, bins, boxes and containers of various descriptions, that held all my quilting stuff, I knew the time had come to put my house (at least the quilting part of it) in order.

Now I used to consider myself a fairly well-organized person. If you had asked me to list my abilities in descending order, organizational skills would be high on the chart. After all, wasn't I a mother who had raised three children, sewed a lot of their clothes, worked part-time and did volunteer work as well? And wasn't it me who used to make sandwiches by the loaf and freeze them, so they would be ready to pop into lunch bags in the morning to save precious time? And I was certainly the one who organized the family's multiple activities with the skill of a veteran field marshal.

In those days, when I had less leisure time than I have now, I couldn't understand the remark of a friend who told me, "I don't have time to get organized." After all, organization was the key to a smooth-running existence.

And I was the same woman now. Or was I?

Then the realization dawned on me. That was all before.

Before piles of fabric began to accumulate; before I acquired stacks of quilting books and magazines; before I bought mountains of batting when it came on sale; before boxes of fabric scraps and unfinished projects began to multiply; before ... yes, before I became a quilter.

Nevertheless, it was time to put into practice the skills that must be lying dormant somewhere in my subconscious. I could do it and I would do it!

But where to begin?

The most obvious place was with the fabric. So I began to empty shelves, boxes, baskets and containers of all kinds with new-found zeal. Aha! Here was the missing fabric. I would just put it aside with the pattern

I needed it for. Now where was the pattern? In an old quilting magazine, I remembered. Perhaps I had better begin to organize the magazines.

After searching several issues and pausing here and there to contemplate interesting projects I might like to make at some future date, I decided to make a note of these. Perhaps I should start a file card system. Yes, that's what I would do. I would go through all the magazines and note the pages of the articles that were particularly interesting or useful. I would begin with the pattern I was looking for. And here it was. I would just put that aside in a "To Do" pile with the rediscovered fabric for future use.

Now then, back to the boxes. Oh, I had forgotten about this. It was a piece of Seminole work I tried as an experiment. There wasn't enough to use in a quilt, but it would make a pretty trim for an apron, if I could just find a coordinating fabric in my stash. I should add that to the pile of "To Do" projects.

And here was the box of odd blocks I had been saving to put into an "anything goes" quilt. Recently, I had come up with the idea of using the odd blocks to make little gift bags. I was sure I had some of the background fabric for those slightly inaccurate freezer-paper blocks. In a bag, inaccuracy wouldn't matter. The borders would even the block up. Another "To Do" project.

And so the day went. All kinds of interesting discoveries came to light. Old neckties, to be made into eye-catching throws; baby blocks to assemble; squares and triangles of various sizes waiting to be sewn into scrap quilts. The "To Do" pile was getting larger and larger.

Before I knew it, the day was gone and I had hardly begun organizing, but that "To Do" pile was exerting such a powerful pull it became obvious to me that the best way to get organized was to finish off all these projects. Or at least try to decrease the number. I had better get started right away.

And then I finally understood what my friend had meant. I didn't have time to get organized.

The Naming of Quilts

$\mathcal{H}$ave you ever wondered how quilt patterns get their names?

Who was the first woman to call her floral pattern Rose of Sharon? Was Old Maid's Ramble named by a disappointed spinster with time on her hands? And was the woman who called her pattern Buzzard's Roost thinking of the bird or her husband?

Quilt names are a source of endless fascination and speculation and there are quilt enthusiasts who have given up quilting altogether to write books on the subject.

Of course some quilt names are self-explanatory and are merely descriptive of the pattern as in Checkered Square, Pyramids, and Diamond Chain. Names such as Jacob's Ladder, Job's Tears (or Troubles), Star of Bethlehem and Cross and Crown are obviously taken from the Bible, while others are named for familiar objects such as Pickle Dish, Secret Drawer, Flower Basket or Spools. Quilts were also named after famous people, for example Lincoln's Platform and Clay's

Choice. And such names as Drunkard's Path, Duck's Foot in the Mud and Snake's Trail, tell us that quilters are not without a sense of humor.

With the thousands of pattern names already used, I was led to wonder if there were any names still available in the unlikely event that I should come up with a new pattern. And I have made the happy discovery that there are still names I could use, and very appropriately, too, for quilts I have made or may yet make in the future.

We are all familiar with "road" names in quilting. There are the Road to Oklahoma, Rocky Road to Kansas and Crossroads to Texas, to name just a few. And isn't there one called the Road to Morocco? (No, sorry. That was a movie starring Bob Hope and Bing Crosby.)

My contribution to the road genre of quilt names would be Road to Ruin. This is the name of a very large quilt made out of expensive fabrics that were bought on impulse without considering how much the whole quilt would cost.

Stars are also very popular as quilt names. Texas Star, Folded Star, Starlight, Oh My Stars are just a few of the variations on this theme. I once designed a quilt which I, highly unoriginally, called Starstruck. As this quilt never got any further than the design stage, I have changed its name to Starstuck.

Many animals have been featured in quilt names. Bear's Paw, Turkey Tracks and Fox and Geese are among the better known. Now, I have plenty of fabrics in my stash which have been waiting a long time to be used and I have found the perfect name for the quilt I should put them in. These are unattractive fabrics that cause me to wonder, every time I look at them, not only why I ever purchased them in the first place, but why I bought so many yards of them. Some of these fabrics have been sitting there for years, waiting for the non-existent matching fabrics or appropriate patterns. It is a relief to think they would be entirely appropriate all together in a quilt called A Dog's Breakfast.

Farming names are very common and Hole in the Barn Door, Churn Dash, Rail Fence and Barn Raising are all well known. Although I've yet to see a quilt called Pigsty, I've seen, and even made, a number of quilts where this title would not be inappropriate.

Similarly, flowers such as lilies, morning glories and the ubiquitous rose have all been featured in quilt names repeatedly. Yet there are lots of unused flower names left to choose from. For example, fleabane and bladderwort, as far as I know, are still available.

And finally there is the well-known Crazy Quilt. Made of hundreds of small pieces, painstakingly stitched together and then hand embroidered and embellished, it was a favorite of Victorian ladies with lots of time on their hands. My version was for a long time a work-not-in-progress. Years ago, when I was but a novice quilter, I began a crazy quilt block on the erroneous assumption that it would be a quick and easy way to use up scraps of fabric. After many abortive attempts to complete this "easy" block, I gave up in total frustration, having come to the conclusion that Absolutely Crazy would apply not only to the quilt, but also to the quilter, should I persevere. (I recently tried this block again with greater success, which has, for a while at least, preserved my sanity!)

I hope these suggestions will help you in your choice of names for future quilts. As for me, I may give up making quilts altogether and have fun just thinking up new names!

A Tale of Two Quilts

$\mathcal{O}$f the many quilts that warmed our beds when we were growing up, it's a pretty blue and white Basket Quilt that I remember best. Each of the twenty baskets contained appliquéd flowers in a variety of patterns, nestled amid soft green leaves. Like most of our family's quilts, it was made (as near as I can place it) in the 1930s. It was given to my mother by my namesake, Ada Parks, my grand-father's housekeeper. Because it was a "good" quilt, used on the bed only when special visitors came, it was one of the few quilts to survive the wear and tear of daily use.

Many years passed after I married and left home, and I forgot all about the blue Basket Quilt. It wasn't until I began making quilts myself that my older brother, who lived a thousand miles from me, told me that the Basket Quilt had been given to him. (He had been a special favorite of Ada Parks.) He and his wife clearly valued it and used it as a summer bedspread, so, as much as I would have liked to own it, I felt I couldn't ask for it. The only alternative was to make a copy for myself.

Peterson's Library
A quilt that went to Show and Tell.

"Show and Tell" *page 25*

Four block blue and pink lap quilt
Four combinations of two little
  blocks make a cozy lap quilt.

"On a Roll" *page 27*

Carlin's Doll Carriage Quilt
Carlin's baby quilt that she literally
   loved to pieces.

PHOTO: MARK WALLACE

"A Natural Combination" *page 30*

Canada Meets Australia
A log cabin quilt in autumn colours:
   the quilt that came full circle.

"Full Circle" *page 118*

A Quilter's Praise—Psalm 148
No need for false modesty here.
   A Quilter's Praise is one of my
   favourite quilts.

PHOTO: BARBARA HEINTZMAN PHOTOGRAPHY

"Down with False Modesty" *page 127*

Crazy Quilt
A successful attempt at making
a crazy quilt.

"The Naming of Quilts" *page 140*

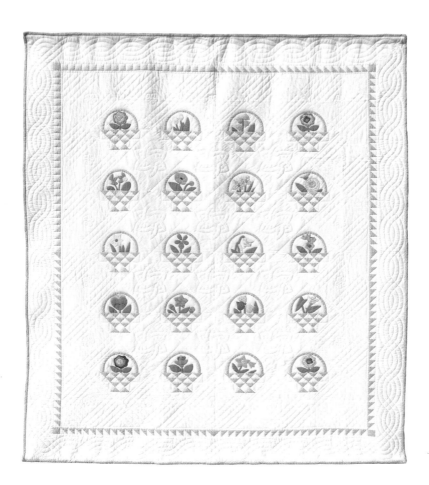

Flower Baskets
My recreation of the original
Flower Baskets quilt.

"A Tale of Two Quilts" *page 144*

Tessellating Butterflies
My answer to a challange.

"The Challenge" *page 162*

For quite some time I looked through pattern books, hoping to find the pattern my namesake Ada had used. Although there were Basket Quilt patterns in abundance, I could find none quite like our original. The nearest I came was a drawing of the same basket block, with the brief direction, "Fill the baskets with pretty flower appliqués." Easier said than done, especially for the novice quilter.

For a while I put the idea of making a copy of the quilt out of my mind. But as my quilting skills improved, I considered the idea of making the quilt from a photograph. My brother agreed to send me a picture of his quilt along with the measurements, so I sent off a long list of questions requesting the information I would need. He, being an engineer, sent me a carefully drafted set of drawings, complete with measurements, for the basket blocks and borders, with the added note, "This is almost as much work as planning a house!"

Now I had the overall dimensions of the quilt and the size of the baskets; but there was still the problem of the flower appliqués. Fortunately, on a visit to my brother, I was able to trace each flower and leaf onto tracing paper, making careful notes as to the color of the fabrics, placement and embroidery embellishment. I discovered that, with the exception of the flowers in the corner baskets, which were alike, all the baskets contained different flowers. Templates had to be made for each leaf and flower part. No easy job to copy!

After all this planning, making the quilt seemed relatively easy by comparison. Having seen the original quilt again, I decided on just two changes: a slight variation in the quilting pattern and the addition of a blue and white binding. (The original quilt just had the white background turned under.) Of course, it was impossible to match the earlier fabrics exactly, especially since they had faded with the years. So my quilt looked much brighter than the original, although I did keep the same colors as much as possible.

By the time I had completed the quilt, my oldest daughter was planning her wedding, and it seemed only natural to give her the quilt as a wedding gift. My brother, who attended the wedding and saw the reproduction for the first time, said, "We did a good job, didn't we?"

Although I have neither original nor copy, I've kept all the patterns and drawings. Perhaps one day, I'll make another copy, just for me.

Vested Interests

$\mathscr{I}$ never, ever, aspired to be a fashion model. When I was young, the world of fashion was as unfamiliar and as distant as that of steeplechasing or brain surgery. Although, if long legs and a skinny body were two prerequisites, there was a time when I would have at least partially qualified. But that was long ago before the skinny body had transformed into ... well, let's not get into that. Suffice it to say, modeling was definitely not for me.

So when it was announced that a fashion show was to be part of the program for our guild's annual banquet, my only thought was, "That should be interesting." The focus of the show was to be vests made in a recent guild workshop, although all quilted garments were welcome. I hadn't attended that workshop, but I did have a vest just finished. But, of course, I had no intention of being one of the models.

Then how did I come to be pirouetting around a room full of quilters, showing off my latest creation?

I have always liked wearing vests. They provide that extra layer of warmth around the body without the bulkiness of sleeves, which sometimes get in the way of doing housework, gardening or, more importantly, quilting. They also serve to coordinate blouses, pants or skirts to make an outfit. They are relatively easy and quick to sew.

I like vests and have made quite a few of them.

The first vest I made as a quilter was the result of a course on using old denim or other fabric scraps to make vests. I enjoyed the process so much (and had so much old denim left over) that I made vests for myself and each of my daughters, as well as a jacket, before I was finished.

One of my favorite vests was made because I wanted to use up some old silk ties I had been given. Like many of my projects, it didn't turn out quite the way I had thought it would. I actually used only parts of four ties and then went into my fabric stash, and then to the fabric store to finish the vest. But I was pleased with the results and also pleased with the compliments I received when I wore it.

My latest vest was made to coordinate with a navy blue skirt I had bought on a trip to the sunny south.

The skirt was a simple ankle-length cotton, gathered at the waist, and with decorative fringing sewn at and above the hemline to give it some style. When I got it home, I discovered, not surprisingly, that nothing in my closet matched it, so, taking the easiest route, I decided to make another vest to go with it.

In my pile of "What am I going to do with these?" fabrics, there was a subdued floral pattern in pale purple and blue on a navy blue background that matched the skirt. It was a good starting fabric. I cut the print into diamonds, which I pieced into four long strips. For the fronts, on each side of the diamond strips, I added other strips of coordinating blues and purples, and in the back, the diamond strips provided a decorative touch to the plain navy blue. For the lining, an unused pyjama jacket, dark blue with a tiny mid-blue stripe, was just the fabric I needed. The vest was quickly finished. A simple shirt top completed the ensemble.

Even though I hadn't taken the guild's course, I thought I might just wear my new outfit to the banquet. Of course, I had no intention of modeling it. It wasn't unusual or distinctive enough for that, I said to myself. On the other hand, if they were short of garments, I might just be asked to lend my vest to fill in. I had better put some information on a card as they had requested, just in case. But I really had no intention ...

I was asked to model the vest and I agreed, although not without feeling a little like a "fool rushing in where angels fear to tread."

As the show proceeded, quilters and garments of various sizes, styles and designs were displayed and admired. None of these ladies looked anything like professional models, but they all seemed to be enjoying themselves. This won't be so bad after all, I thought.

When my name was called, I diffidently rose from my place and began the circuit of the room. Here and there, supportive quilters bolstered my confidence with their encouraging words. "I like your use of color." "Very nice work." "A lovely vest." These and other such phrases raised my spirits.

As I circulated among the tables, the fringes of my skirt swaying and swirling, I began to enjoy myself. I showed the back of the vest, the front, the pyjama lining with its cleverly stitched pyjama pocket to hold the all-important hanky. Encouraging murmurs continued to accompany me as I floated around the room on a cloud of pleasure and satisfaction.

The circuit was almost complete when I noticed a lady leaning slightly toward me.

Another encouraging remark about the vest, no doubt. I moved a little in her direction, so as not to miss a word.

She bent even closer and then, with a simple question, brought me back down to earth.

"Where did you buy your skirt?"

Momentarily taken aback, I named the city.

"Oh," she moaned, "I knew you didn't get it here."

That was it. Back to reality. My brief modeling career was over. I never had any intentions, anyway.

Lost and Found

$\mathscr{T}$idiness is not one of my most outstanding virtues, especially when it comes to quilting. In fact, I think "tidy quilter"is a contradiction in terms. There are neat quilters (all their points match), and there are well-groomed quilters (not a hair out of place), but these descriptions have more to do with personality traits than with the actual process of quilting. The very act of selecting the right fabrics and colors for a quilt necessitates spreading out all the fabrics that might possibly be used in the proposed project on tables, furniture, floor or wherever else you can find space until you actually decide which ones you are going to use. And if, like me, you can't wait to get started on the quilt, and you are not absolutely sure of your choices, the remaining fabrics have to be left conveniently near, so you won't have to search through your stash for them in case you need to reconsider your decisions.

So, right from the start, untidiness is imperative.

Then there's the cutting process. How can you be tidy with selvedges, threads, odd bits and pieces flying from your rotary cutter as you cut and snip and cut some more? Not a chance.

And when you start sewing, there are all those points to snip off and threads to trim, not to mention the seams that sometimes have to be ripped out, creating even more threads. Tidy? Impossible!

That's why, from the time I start a quilt until it is finished, or at least on the quilting frame, my workroom is a place of clutter and mess. I hadn't realized this was an inherited trait until my brother observed one day, "Ada, you're exactly like Mom. Everything is a big mess while you are working at it, then you clean it all up until the next time." Bingo! I thought. You are absolutely right. And luckily, with the realization that untidiness was in my genes, I could relax and just get on with the quilt.

But there comes a time when the quilt is finished. Unused fabrics are finally sorted and put away, the pattern is filed, the vacuum cleaner is brought out and things get back to abnormal again.

I try to get to this stage before my husband and I leave on one of our frequent travels, even if the quilt is not quite finished. After all, I don't want the very nice neighbor who looks in on our place while we are away to see how messy I really am. And who wants to face a big mess after weeks away when you've got so many other things to be attended to? And if I don't come back, what would the people who had to clear up the mess think of me? I do have some self-respect, after all.

Now while this approach to life (i.e., quilting) makes for less time spent on housework and more time spent quilting, I honestly have to admit that it does have one big drawback. And that is: things can get lost in the mess. I thought of this as I went looking for a book I usually keep near me when I'm quilting to write down those absolutely brilliant ideas that may actually develop into quilts or stories about quilts. It was nowhere to be seen. Which was hardly surprising, as every available surface was covered with fabrics, tools and patterns related to my current project. Somewhere buried in all the mess was the book I was looking for. With a little searching, I found it. But it reminded me of a previous time, when I was not so lucky. And the object of my search was not lost in the mess, but lost in the tidiness.

Before an extended trip to the East Coast to visit family, I had decided to take with me some photographs of my daughter's recent graduation to show family members, but I was unable to find the original pictures. Ironically, it was because I had been too tidy and had already put them into a family album, but I didn't discover this until months later. I did find the negatives, however, and I made a special trip to the photo shop to get a second set of prints made just a few days before I was due to leave.

All that week I had been sewing furiously, trying to complete a wall hanging for a charity auction, which was to be held soon after our return. The hanging completed, I did my usual pre-trip cleanup. Fabrics were put back into their bins. Patterns were filed. Books were shelved. The sewing machines were covered and everything was put to rights. Looking at my cutting and sewing tables, I noted how tidy everything looked. Just cutting mats and rulers neatly arranged and a single small pile of books and papers, which I knew I would want to refer to soon after I returned, all tidily stacked in one corner.

With a clear conscience, I packed my suitcase, including a small photo album containing important photos (of quilts) that I wanted to show to special people (those who would appreciate them!) on my travels. And, of course, the photos of my daughter's graduation. I was sure I packed them. So sure that when I went to show them to our family, I knew exactly where they were in the suitcase. Right in with the quilt photos.

To my surprise they weren't there. In disbelief, I searched the whole suitcase—every pocket and zippered compartment was emptied of its contents, but no graduation photos were to be found. Photos of my quilts, yes. Photos of my daughter, no! It was a mystery. They weren't left in my workroom. I had left it very tidy, I knew. Surely I would have seen them there. Likewise, the kitchen, living room, bedroom, etcetera. All were left tidy.

I puzzled over the mystery during the weeks we were away, and as soon as I arrived home I checked all the likely places for those photos, but to no avail. It wasn't until the suitcases were unpacked and put away, the mail sorted, the laundry done and I had time to get back to quilting that the mystery was solved. For there, in that one little pile of papers that I had left so neatly on the end of the table, was the envelope of graduation photos.

There's such a thing as too much tidiness.

Fabrications

 $\mathcal{T}$ he other day, having acquired new shelving, I was rearranging my fabric stash trying to decide what fabrics to put where, when it suddenly occurred to me that I was looking at my fabrics in a new way. Usually, I see pieces of cotton in terms of color or pattern and how they will mix or match in a design I am contemplating. But as I handled them once again, I realized that, in addition to color, pattern and texture, these fabrics also had personalities. They were not just passive inanimate objects waiting for me to select and use them, but, like people, each had individual characteristics that distinguished it from all the others. And, like people, they could generally be classified according to their personalities into broad categories.

For example, in my stash I have fabrics that can only be described as party types. They are loud, bold and colorful and seem to attract other fabrics with the same personalities as themselves. If you begin your quilt with some of these fabrics, they will take right over. They will decide, in no uncertain terms, which other fabrics will join them in the quilting party. And most of those chosen will also be bold and bright. When the quilt is finished, don't try to use it to get a good night's sleep or even for a quick nap; all those vivid hues and striking designs partying together will keep you awake all night. No, the quilts made from these fabrics demand attention. They should be hung on the wall or thrown over a dull sofa or chair, where they can draw attention to themselves. I don't have a lot of these fabrics. They make too much noise in my stash and don't co-operate with me when I try to get them under control.

What you need for a peaceful night's rest is a quilt made from mom-and-pop fabrics. These are two fabrics which are made for each other and go together, as the song says, like "love and marriage" or "a horse and carriage." Put these two fabrics together in the same quilt and they don't need any others. They complement each other beautifully and are perfectly content in a simple pattern such as Irish Chain or Ocean Waves. For people who enjoy making these and other similar traditional patterns, mom-and-pop fabrics make selection a breeze.

Quite the opposite are the orphan fabrics. Despite frequent searches to find a fabric family of which they can become a part, no other fabrics seem the least bit interested in adopting them and they often spend years on their own. Contrary to what you might imagine, even mom-and-pop fabrics show little interest in them. Occasionally, they end up as the backing for a really interesting quilt top, but more often they are left to languish on their own. I have yards of such an orphan fabric. It has been sitting forlornly in a storage box for nearly 20 years. I acquired this fabric in my early years as a quilter, before I became aware of the perils of succumbing to a "buy-one-get-two-free" sale. Not one to pass up what seemed an unbelievable bargain, I came home with six yards of the material, which I confidently expected to be used up in no time. Alas, such was not the case. This fabric was obviously orphaned in the store and its personality so affected that adding it to my stash did nothing to change its basic problems. Periodically I take it out of its box and give it a psychiatric examination, to see if it might benefit from some sort of fabric therapy that might make it useful, but every time I am faced with the same problems and so it goes back in its box once again. A sad case, to be sure.

The wallflower fabrics, on the other hand, are not entirely without hope. Although you may find them in a corner all by themselves, away from the spotlight focused on the more popular fabrics of the day, you shouldn't overlook them. Given the right partners, these shy and somewhat lackluster calicos can blossom into new life and contribute in no small way to a beautiful quilt. They do well in nine-patch blocks, and Rail Fence patterns as a foil for more forceful fabrics. And they often work well with backstage crew fabric types. These are the neutrals: creams, beiges, grays and muted browns—fabrics without which the show could not go on. Although used as a background for the more dominant colors and patterns, they are the fabrics that unite all the rest. Without them there would be no pattern or design. I buy these fabrics often, especially when they go on sale, knowing that I will always find a use for them.

And of course, we can't overlook the debutantes. These are always the latest in the store and in your stash. They have new designs, new color palettes, new names and they "come out" in quite amazing ways in quilts all over the country. Being a debutante is a costly business, so you won't find these fabrics on sale, but treat yourself to a sampling at least. Beware of buying too much, however, unless you know how you will use it. In two or three years—or less—some of these striking debutantes, bereft of their fabric relatives, may well become orphans in your stash.

As I contemplated all these personalities, folded and resting side by side on the newly installed shelves, I wondered if and how they could all be used in the same quilt. The answer was obvious.

In the world of quilting there is one quilt pattern that is appropriate for any fabric and every fabric, regardless of personality.

You've guessed it—a Crazy Quilt.

The Challenge

$\mathscr{I}$t came as a surprise in the mail. A package of four fat quarters from Marilyn, a quilting friend in Australia.

The fabrics were beautiful and the designs were uniquely Australian. Two fat quarters echoed the dot art of the Aboriginal people and the other two featured Australian animals. The colors in all four coordinated beautifully and as I unfolded each piece, admired its design and gently smoothed the folds, I was deeply appreciative of Marilyn's thoughtfulness and generosity. In the enclosed note she wrote, "I'll be interested in what you make from these." As I read these words, I immediately knew that a challenge was before me. What could I make from four unique fat quarters?

From time to time I have been given, or purchased, fabrics I greatly admired and often these fabrics sit in my stash for months and years untouched. Occasionally, I look them over to remind myself what is there or if any of them will suit my current project. More often than not they don't. Then I make a mental note to find a design in which I could use them without destroying their innate beauty. This has been going on for years and still many of the fabrics sit there.

But Marilyn's note issued a challenge I could not ignore. She was waiting to see what I would do with them. If I just left them with the other fat quarters, she would think me unappreciative or perhaps feel that her fabrics held no interest for me. Since she had gone to the trouble to select, package and mail them, I felt the least I could do to show my appreciation was to make them into something useful or decorative or both. Occasionally I mulled over various possibilities, but no inspiration came.

Sometimes fabrics themselves seem to have a voice, and they tell you how they want to be used. You know as soon as you see them what you will make of them. But as I looked at my gift fabrics again and again, no such serendipitous message arrived. These fabrics huddled together silently on the shelf as strangers in a strange land, far from everything they knew.

What *could* I make? It had to be something relatively small but with a distinctive pattern befitting their unique character; but what?

Part of my difficulty was that although the colors of the fabrics coordinated beautifully, they were not ones I would normally choose to work with: deep lime green with blue and red dots, rust, dark red. Only the soft yellows and golds of one quarter fitted my color comfort zone. Then there were the animal designs; they presented a challenge as well. I could not just cut them up into little pieces. I wanted to preserve their identity as much as possible. But I had so little of each design; just one fat quarter. Acquiring more of the same fabrics would be impossible. Even matching them would be a challenge, yet I knew I would need at least one border fabric to complete even a small quilt. So, for months the challenge remained unmet.

Other projects intervened. A queen-sized quilt for a very special family wedding became a top priority. I wasn't intentionally looking for excuses, but smaller projects were easy to finish while I contemplated my problem.

As I was preparing for an extended visit to my daughter, who lives in Houston, I decided the time had come to take up the challenge. No more delays while I thought about what I would do. I had procrastinated long enough. The decision had to be made some time and I was determined that the time was now.

I seldom travel without some sort of quilting project with me and I reasoned that once I decided on the pattern, and if I took only these fabrics with me, I would actually be able to complete at least the top.

An intensive search through various quilt magazines and pattern books ensued, until my eye lit upon a small quilt top in pale pinks and yellows designed by Linda Denner, who had been inspired by the fascinating designs of M.C. Escher. The pastel colors were far from those I intended to use, but it was the tessellated butterflies forming the centre of the design that caught my attention. Tessellations. One of those words I had stored in the back of my mind in the compartment labeled "Ideas I'd like to try someday."

As I studied the pattern, I became more and more certain it would work for my Australian fabrics. The size was right; the design was novel and would challenge me. I could see how the fabrics could be paired for each of two different butterflies and how they would interlock in the pattern. All I would need would be a few small scraps from my stash for the bodies and a border fabric to complete the quilt as a wall-hanging or table-topper. This was it!

After making a test block from scrap fabrics, I realized I was facing more of a challenge than anticipated. Piecing curves required more skill and patience than I had yet acquired. In order for the blocks to lie flat, every section had to fit the adjoining one exactly. I wasn't ready for this, yet neither was I ready to give up the idea altogether. As one who will always try to find the easiest way to sew, I studied the pattern carefully once more and realized that most of the pieces could be joined by overlapping appliqué, a much easier technique and suitable to machining. The remaining pieces could be pieced together as usual.

So, as I packed my suitcase, I tucked in the pattern, the prepared pattern pieces, fabrics and thread to sew them, along with such absolute necessities as my favorite thimble and scissors. The border fabric I hoped to find in Houston. It would give me an excuse (as if I needed one!) to visit some of the lovely fabric and quilt shops there.

No more delays, no more excuses. The challenge would be met.

On the return trip, my suitcase held the finished top and the few remaining scraps of fabric, which I had decided to use as the binding. A week or so later, the quilt, complete with machine quilting, was finished.

As I look at it, I think, Still not my kind of colors, but it looks fine.

I hope Marilyn will like it, but more than that, I'm glad I met the challenge.

How Much Is Enough?

$\int$omeone asked one of the wealthiest men in America this question: "How much money is enough?"

I have often asked myself a similar question when faced with bolts of fabric. "How much is enough? How much shall I buy?" This problem confronts every quilter who has ever been set loose in a fabric shop with hundreds of bolts of beautiful fabrics to choose from and no immediate project in mind.

Of course, there may be quilters who only go to fabric shops when they actually need fabric for a specific project. I have yet to meet such a person, but I can't entirely rule out the possibility that there may be one or two, maybe even three, somewhere in the vast sisterhood of quilters. These people, if they actually exist, have no problem in answering the question above. Before they get to the shop they have chosen the pattern and come armed with a precise list of the yardage they need. Such a quilter probably finds exactly the fabric she is looking for in the first shop she visits. She undoubtedly arrives early in the morning and is the only person there at the time, so she has the undivided attention of the sales assistants and is therefore in and out of the shop before the rest of us have decided which shop to try first. By evening she probably has the fabric washed and ironed and is busy with her rotary cutter on the first pieces.

I really do think there are people like that. In fact I think we have one in our guild. She brought along three large quilts to our September meeting, announcing that these were the most recent of her "make-a-quilt-a-month" projects, which she had finished in the summer. While many of us are happy with making one "block-of-the-month," in the hopes of completing a quilt by the end of the year, these overachievers aim for at least a dozen.

But back to our problem.

Several quilters more-experienced than I am have devised a rule of thumb regarding quantities of a single fabric purchase. So much for a border fabric; so much for a standard quilt top; so much for a baby quilt; and a fat quarter if you just like the fabric, but have no immediate use for it. These guidelines may be fine if you actually know how you are going to use the fabric you buy, but if, like me, you often select fabrics you really like without having the slightest idea of how you will be using them, then the amount to buy becomes a question for which there seems to be no reliable answer.

After years of buying fabric, I've discovered, however, that certain rules seem to operate, in spite of the fog of indecision that often surrounds me in a fabric shop.

Rule 1. If you take your spouse along, you'll buy less fabric than you would on your own. One reason for this is because most men have a shorter attention span in a fabric shop than in a sporting goods store, or, in my husband's case, a bookstore. (One of my most memorable quilt shop visits was in the city where we found a quilt shop next to a bookstore, in which my husband was happy to spend an indefinite period.) He waits to purchase his books until I have arrived on the scene, in case there is something I would like to add, but it wouldn't surprise me if he reads more than one while he is waiting.

The second reason fabric-buying tendencies are suppressed when with one's spouse is that he will know exactly how much you are spending. And unless you are independently wealthy, you want to avoid this kind of revelation in the interests of family harmony.

Rule 2. The marked-down fabrics on the sale table are there for a reason. In spite of their initial appeal—and what quilter can resist a bargain fabric?—be very cautious. That blue, which looks very much like a match for some of the other blues you have at home, is very likely to turn to green or purple the minute it is out the door of the shop. Also, ask yourself if, when you take advantage of the "buy-one-get-two-free" offer, you will really use all six yards of that very unusual orange sunset fabric. If you really need orange sunset fabric, let me know. I have quite a few yards of it myself.

Rule 3. If you are traveling on a shop-hop with other quilters, you will inevitably buy more fabric than you intended, in spite of your iron resolve not to get carried away. No addicted shopper likes to shop alone. So, if by sheer bad luck, you are shopping with a "fabricholic," you need the strength of character of a Daniel to restrain yourself. If she is a shopper with an unlimited budget, don't even go inside the door, unless of course the shop is already crowded with other shop-hoppers. Then you are fairly safe, as the chances of actually being able to purchase what you choose are relatively limited. But be warned, there is something definitely contagious about seeing other women buying fabric.

Rule 4. No matter how much of any one fabric you finally decide to buy, you will not have enough for the project in which you decide to use it. If you buy only a tenth of a yard, you will need at least a fat quarter; if you buy a fat quarter you should have bought a half-yard; if you buy only half, you will need at least a full yard.

Which brings us back to the question, " How much fabric is enough?"

The rich American answered the question for us all when he said of his money, "Just a little bit more."

Fabric Wars

$\mathcal{T}$here they were, lying quietly in their box, just as they had for the past four years. They were fabrics I had collected while on a once-in-a-lifetime trip to Australia and New Zealand four years ago. They were beautiful fabrics, reflecting the landscape, culture, flora and fauna of the countries we had visited. Lovely green fern prints, rich red and brown Maori designs and shell patterns in the luminescent colors of the paua shell reminded me of the rich, almost tropical, vegetation, the beautifully carved exteriors of the Maori meeting houses and the wide sandy beaches of New Zealand. The Australian fabrics featured the bright colors of the native flowers, the dots and swirls of aboriginal designs and here and there a koala print.

From time to time I had taken them out of their box, admired them once again, and had pondered how I could use them in a quilt that would truly be a lasting reminder of a wonderful holiday. Pattern after pattern was considered and discarded for one reason or another.

This quilt had to be both useful and really special—a truly original souvenir. But no inspiration had come and four years later the fabrics were just as I had brought them home.

Now, as I looked at them yet again, I was determined to make something from them. The hunt for a suitable pattern began once more and this time, I decided, I would be a little less choosy. I just wanted to use those fabrics in a simple design that would accommodate them all. No easy task, I admit, considering the vast range of both color and pattern included. However, I came across a pattern I thought would do nicely. Simple to construct and yet, judging by the photograph that accompanied the pattern, any combination of fabrics would look good.

So I took the plunge and began to cut. Large squares were cut into four equal irregular pieces. Pieces of various fabrics were mixed so that each finished block would feature four different fabrics sewn together to form a square.

Finally I had all the blocks put together and was ready to lay them out on my "design wall" (an old flannel sheet pinned to a large piece of cardboard). Carefully placing them side by side, I laid them all out, stood back and took a look. Lo and behold, *disaster*!

Those blocks were a mess. The overall look was appalling. The fabrics that had lain quietly together in their container for four years were now at war with each other. The bright florals were unsuccessfully trying to take over the whole quilt; the more muted cottons were sulking in the background and several pairs of prints placed side by side were steadfastly refusing to have anything to do with each other. This quilt was not going to survive as it was.

There was nothing to be done but to take all the blocks, put them back in the box and go on a long vacation. Which I did. But those fabrics refused to be ignored, surfacing periodically from my subconscious—often when I was trying to have a good night's sleep.

On returning home, feeling somewhat like Pandora, I opened the box again, stared dolefully at the blocks and realized there would never be a Down Under quilt. At least, not until I had picked apart all those carefully sewn pieces, separated the prints and restored them to the comfort of their own kind. Resignedly, I reached for my seam ripper and began the tedious task.

So here I am, back to the drawing board, so to speak. Although the fabrics have lost some of their charm, they are still there, waiting for the perfect pattern. And now they have been joined by gifts of fabric from other parts of the Pacific—Hawaii, Indonesia, Japan.

The Down Under quilt could be a Circle Pacific quilt. Let's see ... circle ... Double Wedding Ring, perhaps? There's an idea! But is it one whose time has come? Only time will tell.

The Sisterhood of Quilters

Somewhere in Edmonton, Alberta, a little child was hurried from her burning home by a firefighter, who immediately wrapped her in a cozy, colorful quilt to protect her against the dangers of shock and the cool outside air. She, no doubt, was glad to cuddle into the warmth of its flannelette backing and, perhaps, was a little cheered by its bright, colorful pattern. The quilt was hers to keep.

If, after the excitement and upheaval of the disaster was over, she looked at the quilt carefully, she would have seen that it was made in a pattern that looked like bows—purple and aqua. A quilter seeing it would immediately recognize it as the familiar Bow-Tie pattern but made in a non-traditional way.

This quilt was available to provide comfort and warmth to a little child in need as a result of that wonderful sisterhood that links quilters all over the world in places as distant as Alaska, Hawaii and Alberta.

This is how it happened.

On a trip to the island of Hawaii one January, I visited a fabric store. (What quilter visiting a new place doesn't?) The store was run by a diminutive lady by the name of Irene Kimura. Although it was near the end of the day, she welcomed me warmly and told me to take all the time I needed.

"I just want to look around," I said.

"Looking is free," she smiled.

Now, turn me loose in a fabric store with hundreds of bolts to choose from and no particular project in mind, and I could be there for hours! Telling me to take all the time I wanted was not going to get me out of there very soon. However, Mrs. Kimura went quietly about her business, while I examined bolt after bolt. I chose and rejected, mixed and matched and eventually came up with my selections, which Mrs. Kimura proceeded to cut for me. As she measured and cut, we chatted. Answering her questions, I told her I was from Canada, a quilter and on a visit to Hawaii.

"Do you know how to do an easy Bow-Tie?" she asked.

Well, I knew how to make a Bow-Tie block and had briefly toyed with the idea of making a Christmas quilt using the Bow-Tie pattern.

"I'll show you," she said. Snipping off a few squares of scrap material, she deftly threaded her needle and began to give me a free quilt lesson. "My son was laid up for a while and he was so bored he made this Bow-Tie quilt," she said, displaying a pretty pink and white lap-sized quilt.

"A lady from Alaska showed me how to do this," she went on, showing me how to stitch the pieces together. It was such a simple procedure: five squares, all the same size, sewn together with only three straight seams. This was my kind of pattern. I watched carefully, so I could remember each step. When she finished, I thanked her and started to pay for the fabric I had purchased, conscious that closing time was imminent. But Mrs. Kimura didn't seem to care.

"You know how to do Flying Geese?" she continued.

"Not your way, I'm sure," I answered.

"I'll show you that one, too."

A few more snips with the scissors. Three rectangles this time. One seam was quickly sewn, the fabric opened out and there was the Flying Geese block. "I make this one a little bit bigger and then I trim to the right size," she said. It looked so easy.

Handing me the sample blocks, she said, "Enjoy the rest of your holiday. Come back again."

Marveling at her generosity of time and knowledge and with grateful thanks, I left the store with my new fabric and my sample blocks.

Back home in Edmonton, I couldn't wait to try the Bow-Tie for myself. I knew just what I would use it for. Our guild had announced that one of its charity projects for the year was to supply the fire department with small quilts they could use to comfort children whose families were victims of fire. The quilts had to be colorful and cozy. I had in my fabric stash a border print, purchased long ago in a two-for-one sale. It had lots of bright purple and aqua. I also had a coordinating calico with a tiny print in the same colors, which was perfect as a background. And among my fabrics, I also found solid purple and aqua. I was off!

In no time (as measured by quilters) I had 48 six-inch blocks cut, pieced and sewn together. The border print set them off perfectly. It certainly looked colorful. Now for the cozy part. A piece of flannelette provided the perfect backing. Machine stitching finished the project and it was taken to the guild at the February meeting.

So, sister quilters in Alaska, Hawaii and Edmonton, thank you, on behalf of a small child in our city who was comforted because of your generosity of spirit. And thank you to all members of our quilting sisterhood, who willingly give of your time, your skills and your efforts that others might be comforted and helped by your quilts.

Quick and Easy No-Cost Quilts

$\mathcal{E}$very quilt maker faces the problem of what to do with the small pieces of fabric left over from the finished quilts. Most quilters, perhaps thinking that they are making a no-cost quilt, use them up in scrap quilts of various patterns and designs. Some very clever quilters, like Karen Combs, author of *Combing Through Your Scraps*, make a career out of designing scrap quilts. Her lovely quilts are an inspiration to those of us with more scraps than we know what to do with. What amazes me about Karen's scraps is that they all work beautifully together. She must have one of the greatest scrap stashes of all time.

Long ago, in my early quilting years, I saw a postage stamp quilt made entirely of one-inch squares of fabric. That was no little project. It was a major undertaking—a full-size quilt containing over 5000 squares, or so we were told in the catalogue description. I didn't stop to count them myself, but I could readily believe it and greatly admired the thrifty quilter who had kept all those tiny pieces and spent many hours, weeks and probably years hand-piecing them all together. Having such inspiration before me, I decided to keep all the many bits and pieces of leftover fabric that making quilts generates, and by piecing these scraps together end up with a no-cost quilt. Of course, knowing my own limitations, I inwardly acknowledged that I probably wouldn't attempt anything so small or time-consuming as the one-inch wonder I had seen, but the virtue—and often the necessity—of being thrifty inspired me to save my scraps.

Well, as every quilter knows, there comes a time when the accumulated scraps threaten to take over the stash. In fact, my stash is often no more than an accumulation of scraps of various sizes. I mostly use them in simple quilts I work on when I've no major undertaking to occupy my time and energy. These leftovers from more elaborate quilts are put in a special box of their own and when I can no longer get the cover on the box, it is time to use some of them up.

So, having finished a large quilt requiring much thought and attention and with no major undertaking in view, I decided to attack the growing pile of fabric pieces.

This was to be an easy project, so I opted for the quickest and simplest design I could find. Because so many of my scraps were strips, it made sense to simply sew the strips onto a long piece of muslin, using the stitch-and-flip technique. This worked fine. It didn't matter whether or not the pieces were all the same width or if they were evenly cut. Even my backing pieces were of different widths. It was going to be an "anything goes" quilt. This would make the final quilt more interesting, I thought, as I would separate all of the pieced strips with black sashing and finish the quilt with a black border and binding. Not very original, but simple to do. Of course I would have to buy the black sashing material, but apart from that (and the batting and the backing and the thread!) I would have a no-cost quilt.

As I sorted through my scraps, I found that some of the strips were quite long and it seemed a shame to cut them into small pieces when I could sew bigger pieces into big blocks much faster. So these pieces were strip pieced diagonally onto large muslin squares.

I accumulated quite a pile of strips and squares (though not quite enough for complete quilts) and my pile of scrap pieces was diminished considerably, when a more important task brought the whole process to a halt and the finished strips and blocks were put away, along with the remaining scraps, into boxes, whose covers now fit quite comfortably.

Needless to say, by the time I started to work on them again, the scrap boxes were once more overflowing. And before I had finished even one of my scrap quilts, certain truths became obvious. For example:

1. Scrap quilts seem like a quick and easy way to use up leftover fabric, but no matter how many scraps you use, you will never use them all up.
2. You will always have to buy more fabric to finish a quilt made of leftover fabrics.
3. You will always have some leftover fabric from the new material you bought.
4. While you have scraps, you will never lack for something to work with.

I haven't had time to get back to the scrap quilts lately, but I know they are there, and any day when I have nothing else to work on, I'll pull out the overflowing boxes and start piecing strips and blocks again. And one of these days—after I buy some more fabric to complete them—I'll finish those quick and easy no-cost quilts.

Time Out

$\mathcal{I}$n that age after the hour glass had passed out of use, but long before digital clocks were invented, I learned to tell the time. That is, I could look at the round face of the clock and tell you what the hands pointing to various numbers meant. I could tell time, but as for being able to explain what time was—ah, that was another matter altogether.

Even now, as a very mature (in years at least) adult, I find it difficult to explain time. The dictionary is of little help, for in spite of its two-column page-long definition, a single succinct meaning continues to be elusive. The first definition given is "duration," a vague and colorless word that is of little help. Ten other meanings and uses of the word "time" follow, but time just won't be pinned down.

Time is a variable quality. It crawls slowly, creeps on, marches along, rushes by, flies and even stands still. You can have all the time in the world, but time waits for no man (or woman). In spite of that, however, you can do a lot with time. You can take time, have a good time, keep time, pass the time, run out of time, even live on borrowed time.

People have long tried to give meaning to time by dividing it into specific periods: seconds, minutes, hours, days, weeks, etcetera. But even this attempt is less than successful, as these divisions have different meanings for different people. Take, for example, a young child enjoying her birthday party with a house full of playmates. The two or three hours allotted by her parents seems far too short, while the same period of time to the adult hosts seems far too long.

Quilters, I'm afraid, do nothing to clarify the various time divisions. We have our own sense of time and every period is longer or shorter relative to our work. For the unaware, I offer these examples.

The smallest measurement of time, a nanosecond, is how long it takes for a quilter to fall in love with a particularly beautiful fabric; it is also how long it takes for a slip of the rotary cutter to ruin that same lovely piece of fabric.

Seconds and minutes are variable periods, depending on how engrossed the quilter is in her work. For example, when the kids call, "Mom, I need ...," a busy quilter will reply, "Just a second." Which means, "I'll be there as soon as I get past this tricky bit of sewing." Similarly, the reply, "I'll be there in a minute," may mean, "when I get this whole block put together," an indefinite time period that will vary with the skill of the quilter and the intricacy of the block.

An hour for a quilter viewing a quilt show is a relatively short period, but for her husband, attending with her, it seems much longer. If he is waiting in the car outside, an hour seems to last forever. If she tells him she will be "an hour or so" at the show, he may as well go enjoy a movie or a baseball game. It won't be too long for her.

Many quilters think they know how long a day is. But even among quilters, this time period varies considerably. Those who publish quilt-in-a-day patterns, obviously have longer days than the people who buy their books and try to make the quilts.

A week is the ideal amount of time for a quilt conference/show/retreat. If it includes a "quilt shop-hop," however, or if the quilter has taken a particularly challenging class, it may seem a little short.

A year is the approximate time it takes (for me, at least) to piece and hand-quilt a queen-sized quilt.

Eternity, to a quilter's spouse, is the length of time he spends waiting for his wife in the fabric store. To his wife, it is the amount of time required to make all the quilts she wants to sew.

So you see, although it is impossible for a quilter to be as precise about time as she is about her piecing, time is very important none the less, because the dedicated quilter, when she is practicing her art, is having the time of her life.

Thirty Things I Learned from Making Quilts

1. Patience.
2. If you love what you're doing it isn't work.
3. Going to pieces can be the beginning of something new and better.
4. Patience.
5. Doing things right the first time is much easier than correcting mistakes.
6. I should have paid more attention in math classes.
7. My most useful tool is a seam ripper.
8. Patience
9. Bargain fabric isn't always a bargain.
10. No finished quilt is a failure.
11. Quilt police won't get me if my stitches aren't even.
12. There is no likelihood of a quilter running out of ideas for quilts.
13. If your quilt needs perking up try adding some black.
14. Masking tape is a valuable quilting tool.
15. A finished quilt will always find a home.

16. All greens go together in nature and in quilts.

17. Patience.

18. Babies can't tell the difference between a quilt that has been hand pieced and quilted and one that has been made from a quilted panel.

19. Often, neither can their mothers.

20. Neither of them care.

21. If you want to give someone a special gift, give them a quilt. (If they let their dog sleep on it don't give them another one.)

22. If you want to give them the gift of a lifetime, teach them to quilt. (Then they'll feel really sorry they let their dog sleep on your quilt.)

23. Patience.

24. There is always something new to learn in quilting.

25. Your own saliva on a little piece of cotton will make your own blood stains disappear from cloth.

26. A tidy sewing space is the sign of an absent quilter.

27. There is more than one way to thread a needle.

28. A quilter can't have too much fabric or too large a work space.

29. No one who loves quilting has ever finished making all the quilts she would like to.

30. Patience.